Structural Hearing

TONAL COHERENCE IN MUSIC

Structural Hearing

TONAL COHERENCE IN MUSIC

VOLUME TWO

BY FELIX SALZER

WITH A FOREWORD BY LEOPOLD MANNES

DOVER PUBLICATIONS, INC. • NEW YORK

Acknowledgments

Grateful acknowledgment is made to the following publishers for permission to use
  copyrighted material:
Associated Music Publishers, Inc. (Ex. X, 410, 411, 445, 453).
Boosey & Hawkes, Inc. (Ex. 239, 241, 377, 386, 406, 407, 412, 416, 419, 452).
Elkan-Vogel Co., Inc. for Durand et Cie. (Ex. 290).
Leeds Music Corp. (Ex. 380, 451).
E. B. Marks Music Corp. (Ex. 413).
Oxford University Press, Ltd. (Ex. 319, 331).
Salabert, Inc. (Ex. 414).

I wish, furthermore, to thank the following for permission to reprint material from their
  publications:
Harvard University Press, for various quotations from *Historical Anthology of Music;
  Oriental, Medieval and Renaissance*, Vol. I, Revised edition, 1949 (Ex. 184, 185, 510,
  513, 515, 524, 525).
E. B. Marks Music Corp. for Ex. 415.
Oxford University Press, Ltd. for Ex. 209.
G. Schirmer, Inc. for Ex. 418 and for the excerpts from Ruth and Thomas Martin's
  translation of *The Magic Flute* (Ex. 483).
F.S.

Contents

Notes to the Reader

Ideally, a book of this type would present every musical quotation discussed, along with its voice-leading graphs. This proved impractical for reasons of space; therefore, the following plan has been adopted. With very few exceptions the examples in Part I, Part II through Chapter Six and in Part III appear in complete form (music and graphs). In Chapter Seven the music has been omitted for most quotations from standard literature and for the quotations of large excerpts. Chapter Eight, which deals with complete compositions, offers exclusively voice-leading graphs without the music. Since all the music omitted is from available editions, it is hoped that this procedure will not be disadvantageous to the reader.

It has been found practical to print many examples and their graphs (especially the larger ones) running across facing pages, in order to make the course of voice leading clearer for the eye, and to avoid awkward turning of pages as much as possible. The first such example is Ex. X. If there is doubt about the continuity, the reader is advised to orient himself by means of the measure numbers.

In the quotations from music of earlier times, treble and bass clefs have been consistently used, even if the transcriptions in the indicated sources do not follow this procedure. Furthermore, in some compositions, transpositions and change of note-values have been carried out, thus reverting to the readings of earlier sources.

List of Musical Illustrations

Notes and Glossary for the Voice-Leading Graphs

1. The note-values indicate the structural value and significance of tones and chords; they do not indicate rhythmic values.

2. The difference in structural significance is given in four different note-values: half-notes, quarter-notes, notes without stem and occasionally eighth-notes. The latter are used to indicate embellishments and appoggiaturas. The highest note-values in a graph represent tones or chords of the highest structural order. Among notes of equal value, those whose stems reach the same level are of the same structural order.

3. The relation between identical and different tones or chords, and specifically their structural connection, is indicated by dotted or solid slurs and lines, curved or horizontal arrows or by beams.

4. Horizontal, solid arrows (used mostly in regard to bass motions) indicate the direction or driving tendency of the music in general, or passing motions in particular.

5. A note in parenthesis with or without a dotted stem means a note expected on the basis of direct voice leading, but omitted or substituted for in the composition.

6. Brackets of various kinds indicate either chord prolongations ‿‿‿ or melodic parallelisms ⌐——⌐ .

7. Roman numerals are assigned to harmonic chords only; the relative size of these numerals corresponds to their structural value.

8. A small Roman numeral in parenthesis indicates the chord of harmonic emphasis.

Glossary of Symbols

P	Passing tone or passing chord
N	Neighbor note or neighbor-note chord
UN and LN	Upper and lower neighbor note
IN	Incomplete neighbor note
$\frac{N}{P}$	Neighbor-passing chord
Em	Embellishing chord
CS	Contrapuntal-structural chord
DF	Double function chord
M	Mixture
||	Interruption
D	Dividing dominant
A B or A B A[1]	Indication of form

List of Sources (*Abbreviations*)

AM   *Altniederländische Motetten,* ed. by W. Braunfels. Oratori-
umsverlag, Köln.

AMI   *L'Arte musicale in Italia,* ed. by L. Torchi. G. Ricordi e C.,
Milano.

AUDM   *Aufführungspraxis der Musik,* by R. Haas. Akademische Ver-
lagsgesellschaft Athenaion, Potsdam.

CM   *Cent Motets du XIIIᵉ Siècle,* transcribed by P. Aubry. Rouart,
Lerolle & Cie., Paris.

DAS CHORWERK   *Das Chorwerk,* ed. by F. Blume. G. Kallmeyer
Verlag, Wolfenbüttel.

DTOE   *Denkmäler der Tonkunst in Oesterreich.* Artaria & Co., Wien.

HAM   *Historical Anthology of Music; Oriental, Medieval and
Renaissance Music,* ed. by A. T. Davison and W. Apel,
Vol. I. Rev. ed. Harvard University Press, Cambridge,
Mass.

HDM   *Handbuch der Musikgeschichte,* ed. by G. Adler, 2nd ed.
Heinrich Keller, Berlin.

EPM   *The Evolution of Piano Music (1350–1700),* ed. by C. Sachs.
E. B. Marks Music Corp., N. Y.

MET   *Music of Earlier Times (13th Century to Bach),* ed. by J.
Wolf. Broude Bros., N. Y.

MMA   *Music in the Middle Ages,* by G. Reese. W. W. Norton & Co.,
N. Y.

MW   Guillaume de Machaut, *Musikalische Werke,* ed. by F. Lud-
wig. Breitkopf & Härtel, Leipzig.

OHM   *The Oxford History of Music.* Oxford University Press, Ltd.,
London.

OL   Orlando di Lasso, *Sämtliche Werke.* Breitkopf & Härtel,
Leipzig.

SHM   *A Short History of Music,* by A. Einstein. 2nd ed. Alfred A.
Knopf, N. Y.

TC   *Sechs Trienter Codices*, ed. by G. Adler. In DTOE.

VDO   *Studien zur Vorgeschichte der Orchestersuite im 15. und 16. Jahrhundert*, by F. Blume. Kistner & Siegel, Leipzig.

WJO   Jacob Obrecht, *Werken*, ed. by J. Wolf. Johannes Müller, Amsterdam.

WJP   Josquin des Prés, *Werken*, ed. by A. Smijers. G. Alsbach & Co., Amsterdam.

Note: Sources for the quotations from English virginal compositions, which have been repeatedly reprinted, are omitted.

Musical Illustrations

I
BACH Prelude No. 21 (Well-Tempered Clavier, Bk I)

II
BACH Chorale (No. 294)

III BACH Chorale (No. 23)

a applied Dominant · passing chord

I ⟶ II⁶₅ V I

b N P

I ⟶ II⁶₅ V I

c I II⁶₅ V I

IV

a

b

c

d

e graph III a

f chorale

SCHUBERT Waltz, Op 18, No. 10

VI

horizontalization of

VII

VIII MOZART Piano Sonata, A minor, K. 310

5

IX

X HINDEMITH Piano Sonata No. 3

6

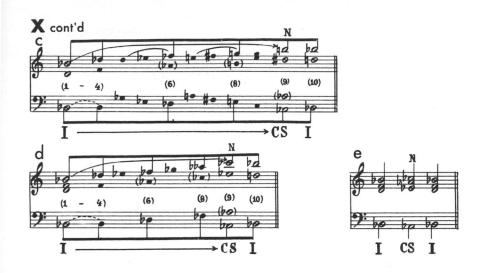

1   BACH Chorale (No. 6)

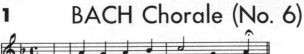

a

2   D. SCARLATTI Sonata, D minor, L. 413

a

becomes

b

3   BEETHOVEN Bagatelle, Op 119, No. 11

Andante, ma non troppo

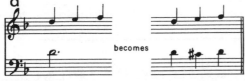

a

4

5 SCHUMANN Little Piece (Album for the Young)

6 SCHUBERT Waltz, Op 9, No. 8

7 **HAYDN Minuet**

8 **FOLK TUNE**

9 **SCHUMANN Album-Leaves, Op 124 No. 16**

10 **BEETHOVEN Piano Sonata, A Major, Op 2, No. 2**

a

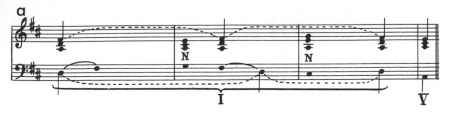

11   BACH Chorale (No. 7)

a

horizontalization of

b

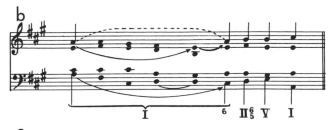

c

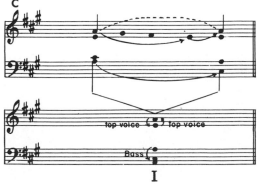

18

19

20

21

22

23

24

a

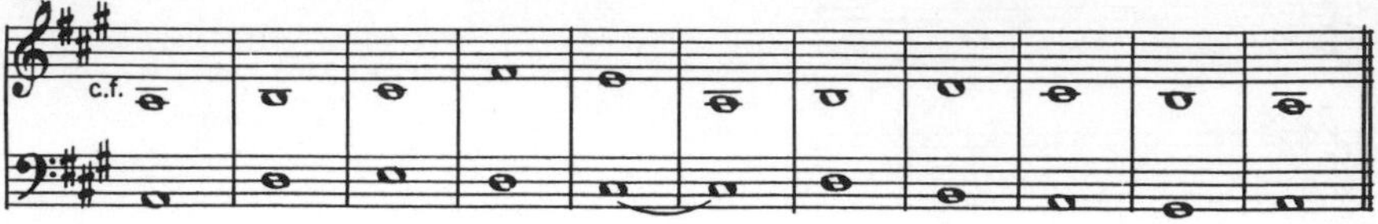

b

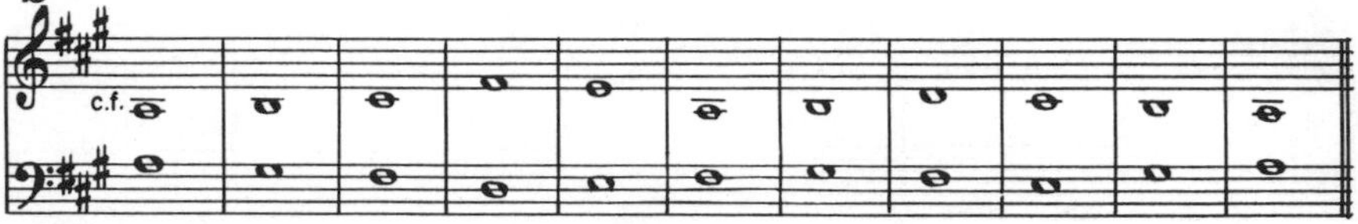

25

a b

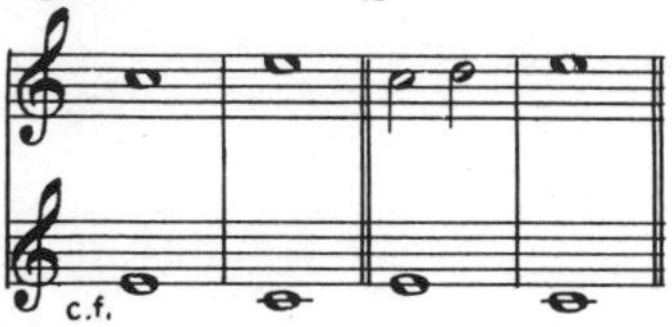

26

a b

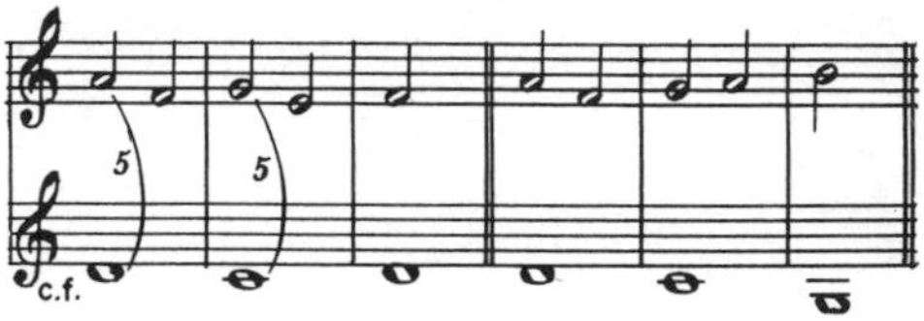

27

a b

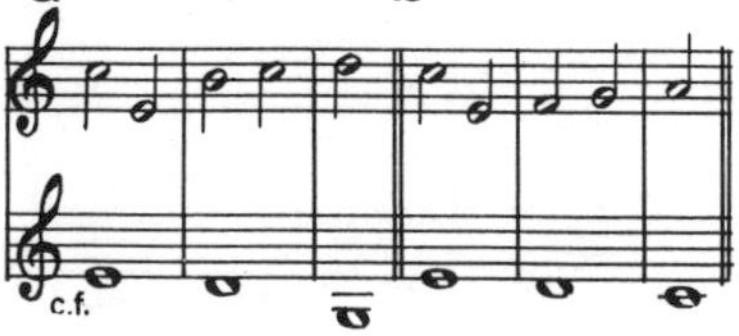

28

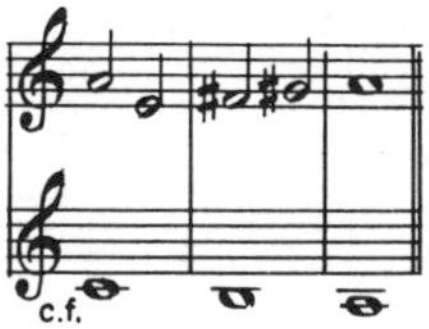

29

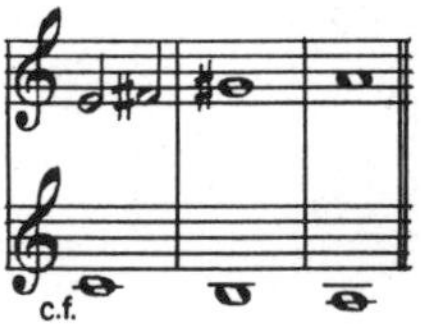

30

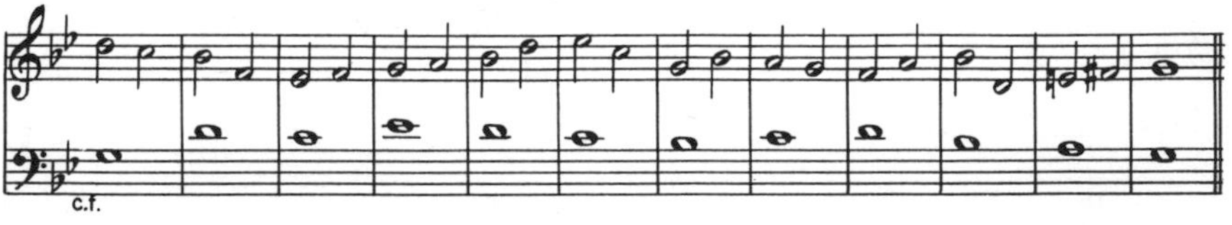

31

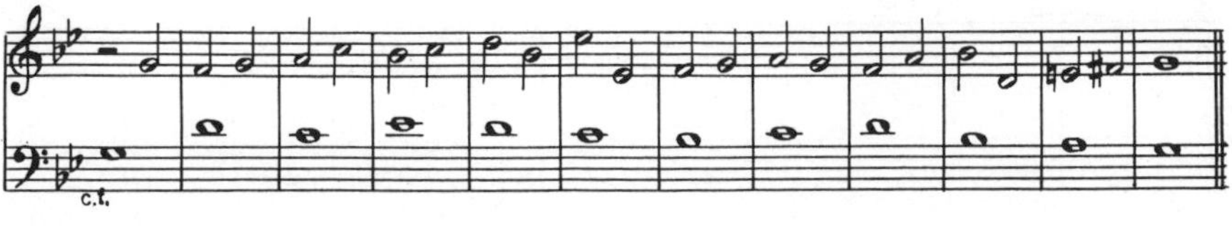

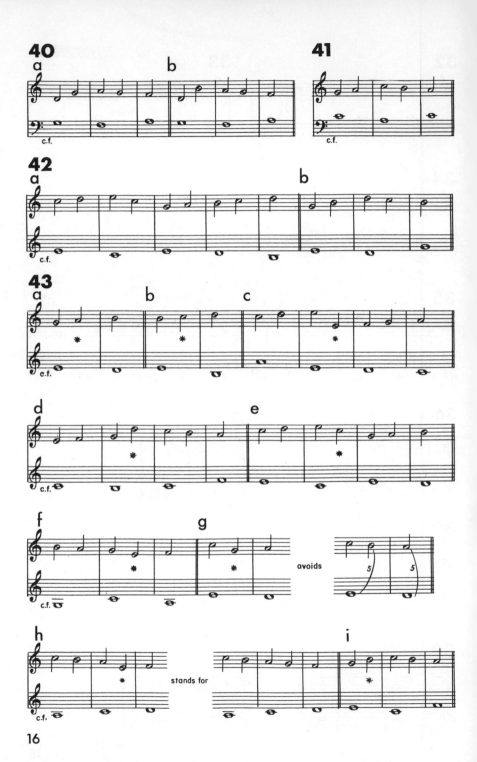

44

45

46

a   b   c   d

47

a   b

48

a   b

49

a progression   b embellishment

50

51

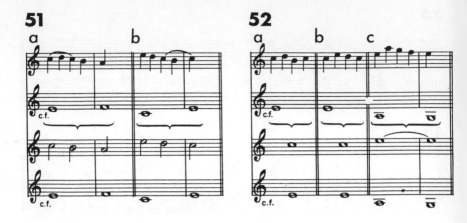

52

53   **54**

18

55

56

57

a

b

19

58

59

60

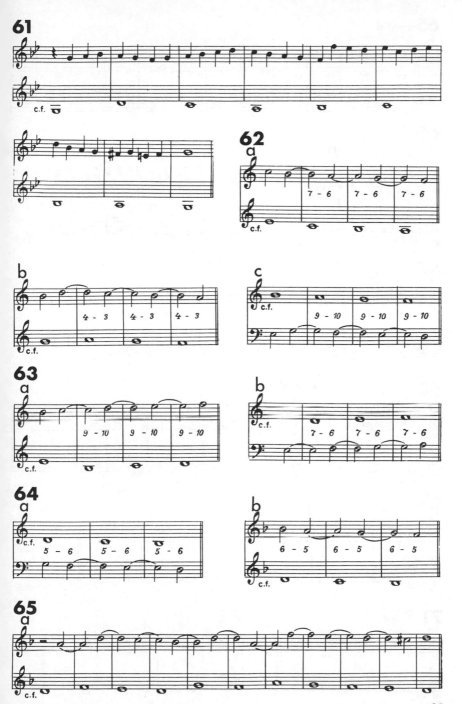

21

73

74

75

76

77

78

23

79

80

81

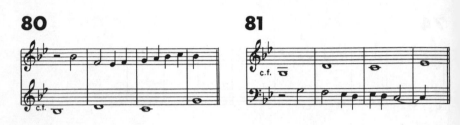

82

83

84

85

86

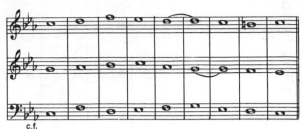

c.f.

87

c.f.

88

c.f.

89

c.f.

25

90

91

92

93

26

94

95

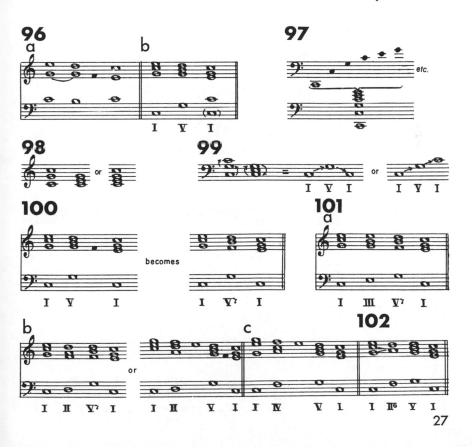

Part II Chapter Four

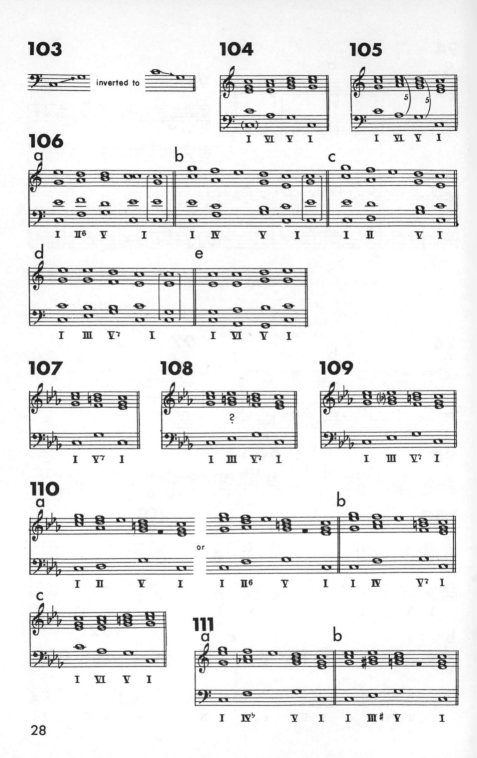

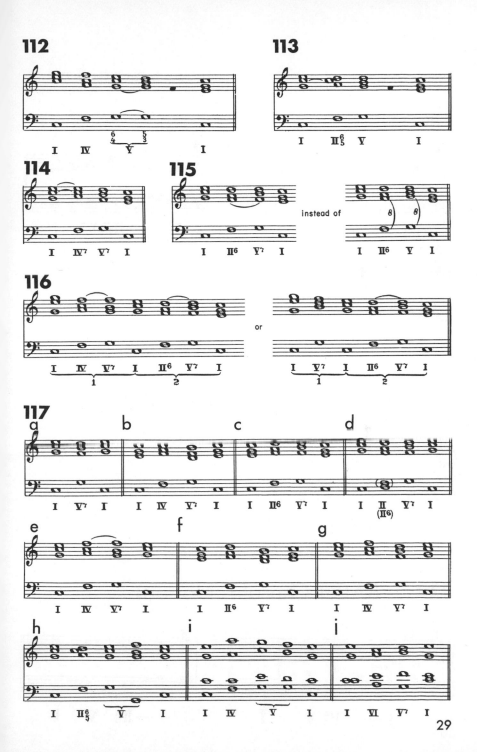

29

118

I ⟶ II⁶ V⁷ I

I ⟶ II⁶ V⁷ I

I ⟶ II⁶ V I

119 BACH Chorale (No. 337)

I ⟶ II⁶₅ V⁷ I

120 BACH Chorale (No. 88)

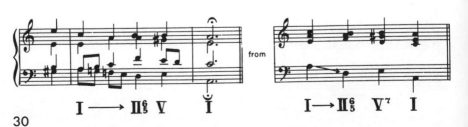

I ⟶ II⁶₅ V I

from

I ⟶ II⁶₅ V⁷ I

121

$I \longrightarrow II \ V^7 \ I$ or $I \longrightarrow II \ V^7 \ I$

122 BACH Chorale (No. 348)

$I \longrightarrow II \ V \quad I$

123

BACH Chorale (No. 246)

$I \longrightarrow II^6_5 V \ I$

a

$I \longrightarrow II^6_5 V \ I$

124

$I \longrightarrow V^7 \quad I$

125

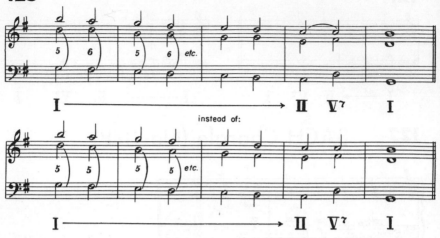

instead of:

126

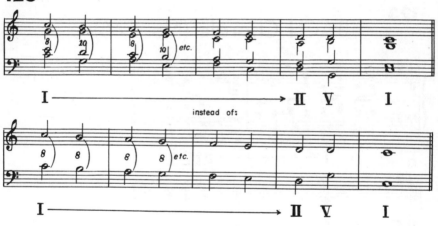

instead of:

127
a

127 cont'd

128

from

129

33

130

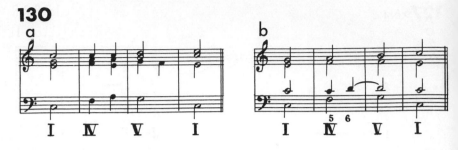

131 CHOPIN Waltz, Op 34, No. 2

132 BACH Gavotte (French Suite No. 5)

133 BRAHMS Piano Sonata, F minor, Op 5

136 cont'd

137

138

139

140 BACH Chorale (No. 330)

141 SCHUBERT Waltz, Op 50, No. 1

142 CHOPIN Waltz, E Major (Posth.)

Tempo di valse

143 MOZART Piano Sonata, C Major, K. 545

Allegro

144 SCHUBERT Ländler Op 67 No. 5

145 BACH Chorale (No. 346)

146

a

b

I   II⁶₅ V⁷   I   I   II⁶₅ V⁷   I

BACH Little Prelude, C minor

152 BACH Prelude No. 1 (Well-Tempered Clavier, Bk I)

153

154 C. P. E. BACH Minuetto

155 CHOPIN Waltz, Op 69, No. 2

156 JOSQUIN Missa: Pange lingua

Et in - car - na - tus est
Et in - car - na - tus est
Et in - car - na - tus est
Et in - car - na - tus est

[From DAS CHORWERK, Vol. I]

157

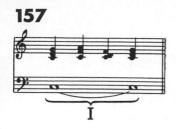

158 BACH Prelude No. 6 (Well-Tempered Clavier, Bk I)

159

160 BACH Chorale (No. 11)

160 cont'd

161

162 BACH Chorale (No. 366)

163 BACH Chorale (No. 367)

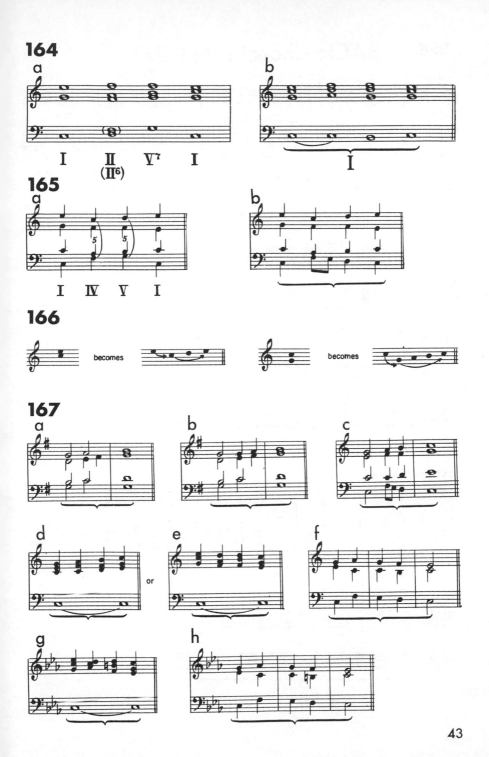

43

168 BACH Chorale (No. 24)

169 BACH Prelude No. 2 (Well-Tempered Clavier, Bk II)

170 BACH Little Prelude, F Major

171

171 cont'd

172

173

174 BACH Chorale (No. 233)

I   V   I

175 BACH Chorale (No. 367)

I   II⁶₅ V I

176 BACH Chorale (No. 362)

I   II⁶₅ V I

177 BACH Chorale (Peters No. 118)

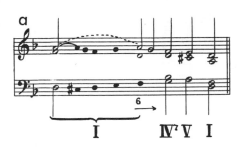

a

I   IV⁷ V   I

b

I   →   IV⁷ V   I

178

a

I   II⁶

b

I   II

c

I   II⁶

179 BACH Chorale (No. 110)

a

I   IV⁶   V   I

b

I   IV⁶   V   I

180

a

b

181

a

I   IV⁷ V   I

b

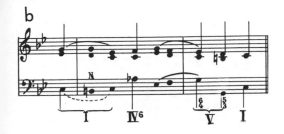

182 BACH Chorale (No. 42)

a

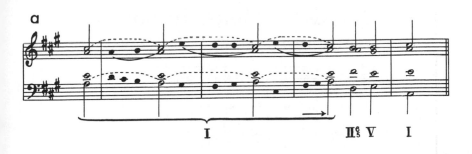

b

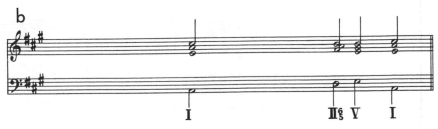

183 MOZART Piano Sonata, D Major, K. 311.

184 JOSQUIN Motet: Tu pauperum refugium

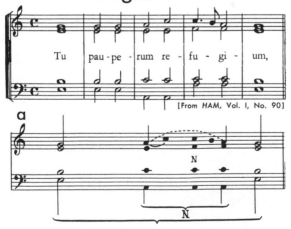

Tu pau - pe - rum re - fu - gi - um,

[From *HAM*, Vol. I, No. 90]

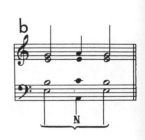

185 ## GIACOMO FOGLIANO Ave Maria

San - cta Ma - ri - a, Ma - ter De - i, o - ra pro no - bis

[From *HAM*, Vol. I, No. 94]

186 ## BARTÓK Piano Pieces for Children, No. 32

Allegro ironico

186 cont'd

187

188

52

189

a

$$\text{I} \qquad \text{IV}^6 \qquad \text{V} \qquad \text{I}$$

b

$$\text{I} \qquad \text{IV} \qquad \text{V} \qquad \text{I}$$

190

a

 or

$$\underset{\text{I}}{\overset{\frac{4}{3}}{}} \longrightarrow \text{II}^6 \; \text{V}^7 \quad \text{I} \qquad\qquad \underset{\text{I}}{\overset{6}{}} \; etc.$$

b

 from

$$\text{I} \longrightarrow \text{II}^6_5 \; \text{V}^7 \quad \text{I} \qquad\qquad \text{I} \quad \text{P} \quad \text{II} \; etc.$$

191

192

193

194

55

194 cont'd

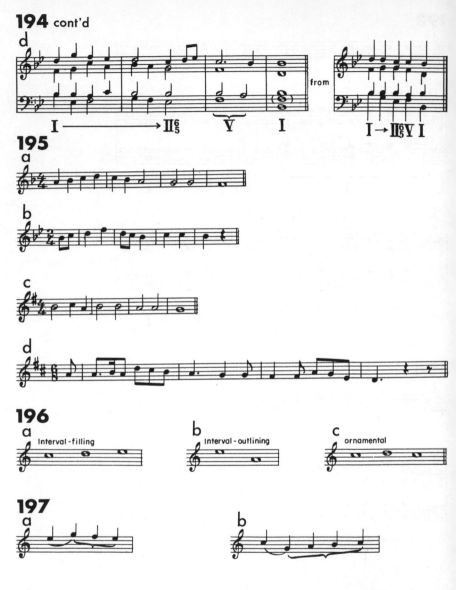

195

196

197

198 MOZART Piano Sonata, F Major, K. 280

199 MOZART Piano Sonata, C Major, K. 279

200 BACH Courante (Partita No. 5)

a  from

201 MOZART Piano Sonata, C Major, K. 279

a

202 HANDEL Double

203 MOZART Rondo, A minor, K. 511

204

205 MENDELSSOHN Song Without
Words, Op 62, No. 1

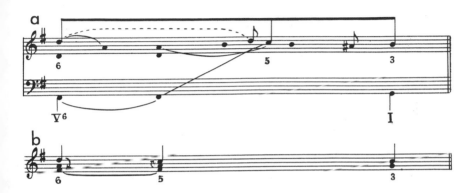

206 BEETHOVEN Piano Sonata,
F minor, Op 2, No. 1

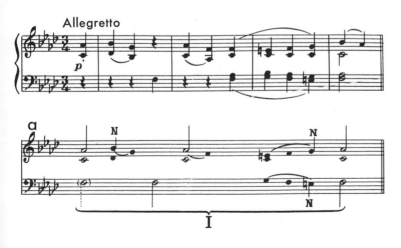

207 MOZART Fantasia, D minor, K. 397

208 MOZART Piano Sonata, C minor, K. 457

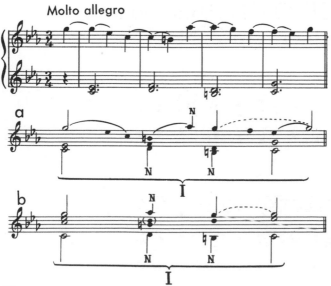

209 CARISSIMI Cantata: Mary Stuart

Ah mo - ri - re, ah mo - ri - re, ah mo - ri - - - - - re

[From OHM, Vol. III]

210 HAYDN Piano Sonata, C Major, No. 35

Allegro con brio

210 cont'd

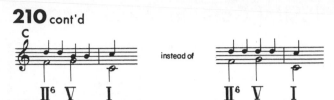

instead of

II^6 V I II^6 V I

211   HAYDN Piano Sonata, D Major, No. 19

212   FROBERGER Suite: "Auf die Mayerin"

[From *DTOe*, Vol. VI]

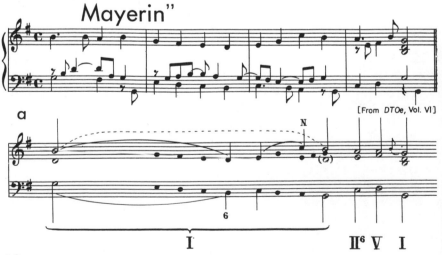

213 MOZART Courante (Suite, K. 399)

I   II V I II⁶→V I   I II⁶→V I

214 HAYDN Piano Sonata, G Major, No. 27

I   II⁶   V   I

215 FOLK TUNE

I   II⁶   V   I

216   CHOPIN Nocturne, Op 32, No. 1

217   MOZART Piano Sonata, F Major, K. 280

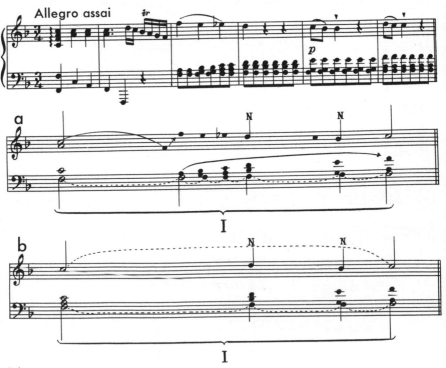

218 MENDELSSOHN Song Without Words, Op 102, No. 2

219 MOZART Aria ("Don Giovanni")

219 cont'd

quel - che a lei pia - ce, ___ vi - ta mi _ ren - de, etc.

220 CLEMENTI Sonatina, G Major, Op 36, No. 2

221 BEETHOVEN Piano Sonata,
E Major, Op 109

222 BEETHOVEN Symphony No. 9

223 SCHUBERT Ländler, Op 18, No. 2

a

b   becomes

c

I V I

224 C. P. E. BACH Fantasia

a   N

b

225 BACH Praeludium (Partita No. 1)

a

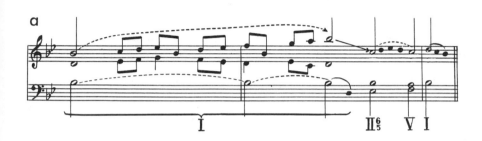

226 BEETHOVEN Piano Sonata,
G Major, Op 79

Presto alla tedesca

226 cont'd

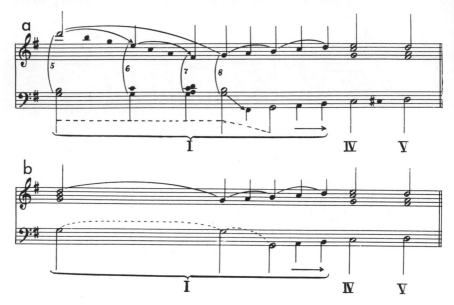

227 HANDEL Variation 1 (Air from Suite No. 3)

228 BACH Courante (Suite pour le clavecin, E♭ Major)

229 BEETHOVEN Piano Sonata, E Major, Op 14, No. 1

229 cont'd

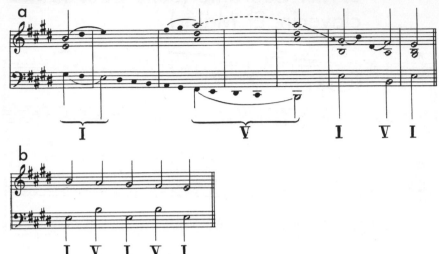

a

I   V   I   V   I

b

I V I V I

230   MOZART Trio, E♭ Major, K. 498

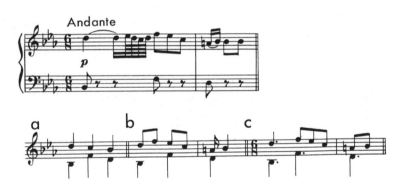

Andante

p

a   b   c

231   BACH Praeambulum (Partita No. 5)

a

a4 9 7 ♯5
C⁶

C⁶

232 BACH Aria variata

233 MOZART Piano Sonata, C Major, K 545

234 SCHUMANN Melody (Album for the Young)

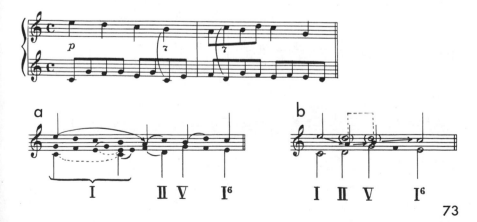

235 MOZART Fugue, C Major
(Fantasia, K. 394)

a

which avoids

236 BACH Chorale (No. 64)

a

10   8   6

237 BACH Chorale (Peters No. 43)

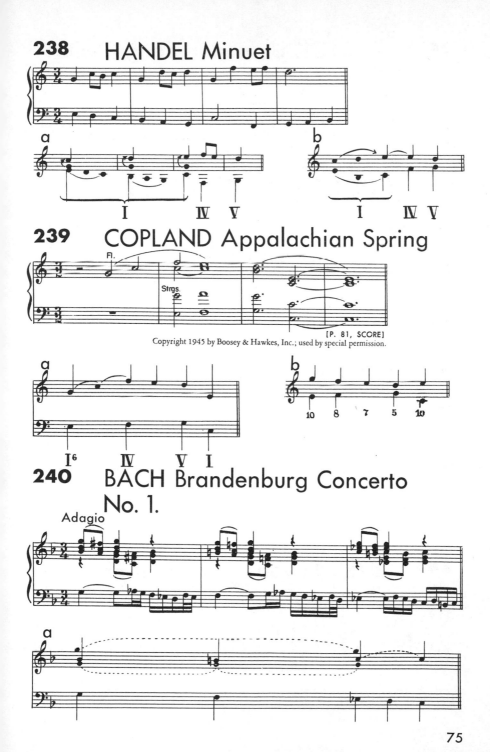

238 HANDEL Minuet

a

I IV V

b

I IV V

239 COPLAND Appalachian Spring

Fl.

Strgs.

[P. 81, SCORE]

Copyright 1945 by Boosey & Hawkes, Inc.; used by special permission.

a

I⁶ IV V I

b

10 8 7 5 10

240 BACH Brandenburg Concerto No. 1.

Adagio

a

241 BARTOK Ukrainian Song (Petite Suite)

Allegretto

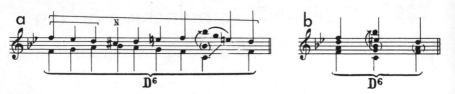

a

N

D^6

b

D^6

242

a

5 6   7 6   7 6   7 6

b

5 6   5 6   5 6

c

9 10 9 10 9 10

243 BYRD Pavane: The Earle of Salisbury

244 MOZART Piano Sonata, G Major, K. 283

245 GOTTLIEB MUFFAT Air (Suite, B♭ Major)

246 BACH Prelude No. 10 (Well-Tempered Clavier, Bk I)

247 HAYDN Piano Sonata, C Major, No. 21

248 MOZART Piano Sonata, G Major, K. 283

249 BACH Little Prelude, C minor

250 CHOPIN Mazurka, Op 41, No. 4

251 CHOPIN Etude, Op 25, No. 5

252 SCHUMANN Kreisleriana, Op 16, No. 8

253

254 BEETHOVEN Piano Sonata, G Major, Op 14, No. 2

254 cont'd

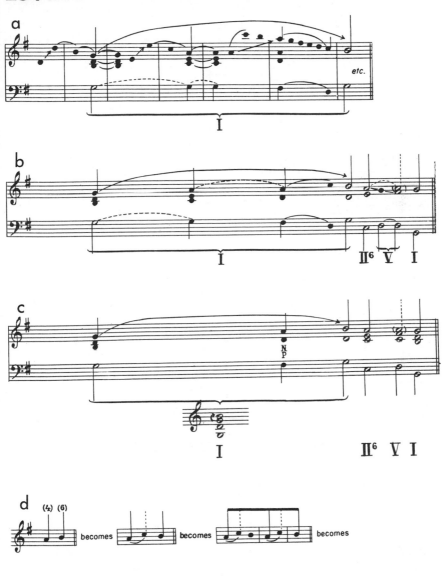

255

256

257

258

259

260

261

I II⁶ V I

262

I IV V I

263

I II⁶ V I

86

263 cont'd

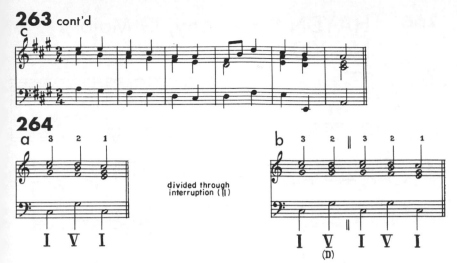

264

a   3 2 1

divided through
interruption (‖)

I   V   I

b   3   2 ‖   3   2   1

I   V   I   V   I
(D)

265 BEETHOVEN Piano Sonata,
E Major, Op 14, No. 1

Allegretto

a

see meas. 1–6

I   V   I   V   I
(D)

266 **HAYDN Symphony, G Major, No. 100**

a

I V I

I II V ‖I V I II⁶ V I
(D)

267 **MOZART Quartet ("Don Giovanni")**

Andante

Non ____ ti fi-dar, o mi-se-ra, di quel ri-bal-do cor!

Me già tra-dì quel bar-ba-ro, te vuol tra-dir an-cor!

267 cont'd

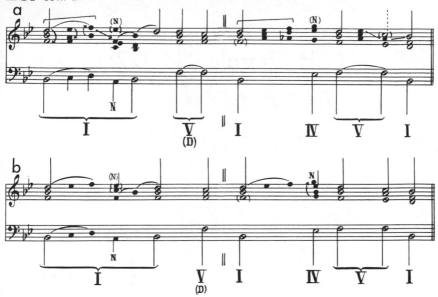

268   BASSE DANSE

[From VDO, App. P. 35]

269 BACH Chorale (No. 192)

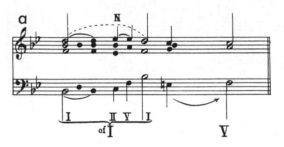

I   II V I
of I   V

270

I

271 GIBBONS The Queene's Command

I   V
     (D)   I V I   I   V I

272 HAYDN Piano Sonata, E♭ Major, No. 52

JOSQUIN Motet: Ave Maria

[From AM, P. 9]

a

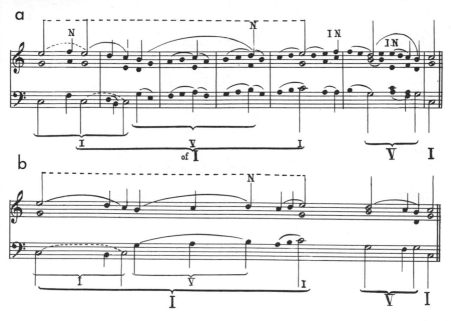

b

274   CLÉREAU Missa: In me transierunt

[From HDM, Vol. I, P. 330]

a

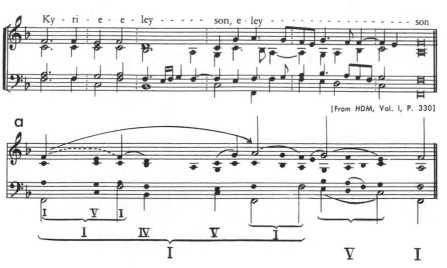

275

276 BACH Chorale (No. 5)

277 MOZART Piano Sonata, D Major, K. 576

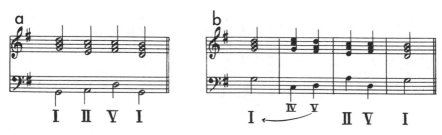

278

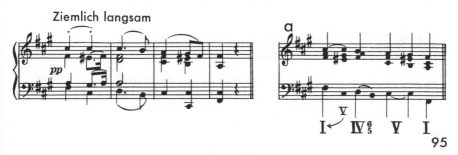

279 SCHUMANN Bunte Blätter, Op 99

280 BACH Prelude No. 7 (Well-Tempered Clavier, Bk II)

a

I ←→ V   II V I

281

a   b

I ←→ V IV V I   I ←→ V II V I

282 SCHUBERT Ländler, Op 18, No. 10

V → I

283 CHOPIN Etude, Op 10, No. 4

V → I

284 CHOPIN Mazurka, Op 63, No. 2

285 CHOPIN Mazurka, Op 24, No. 3

286 SCHUMANN Der Nussbaum

287 # SCHUMANN Dichterliebe, No. 5

288 # BEETHOVEN Piano Sonata, Eᵇ Major, Op 31, No. 3

289 # BEETHOVEN Piano Sonata, Eᵇ Major, Op 81a

290 # RAVEL Rigaudon (Tombeau de Couperin)

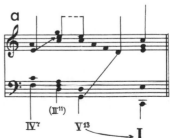

291

292

293 SCHUBERT Waltz Op 127, No. 3

294 **SCHUBERT Piano Sonata,**
D Major,

295 **SCHUBERT Waltz, Op 10, No. 6**

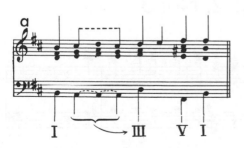

296 SCHUMANN Humoreske, Op 20

297 CHOPIN Waltz, Op 64, No. 2

298 BEETHOVEN Piano Sonata, C Major, Op 2, No. 3

299 SCHUMANN Fantasiestücke, Op 12, No. 3

300 LISZT Liebestraum (Nocturne No. 3)

Poco allegro, con affetto

301

302

303 ## SCHUMANN Scenes from Childhood, Op 15, No. 1

304 ## CHOPIN Mazurka, Op 17, No. 2

SCHUMANN Album-Leaves, Op 124, No. 10

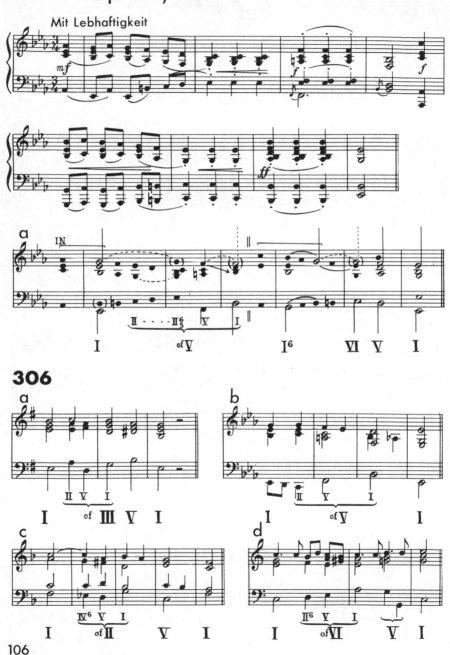

306

307 SCHUMANN Album-Leaves, Op 124, No. 5

308 BRAHMS Intermezzo, Op 118, No. 2

309

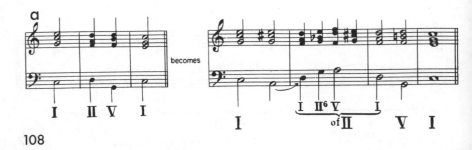

309 cont'd

310 SCHUMANN Auf dem Rhein

311 CHOPIN Mazurka, Op 59, No. 2

312 BACH Chorale (No. 55)

313 BACH Chorale (No. 177)

a

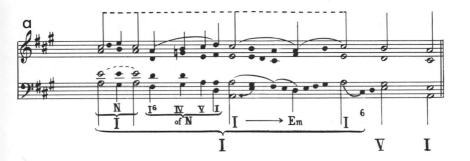

$$\text{N} \quad \text{I}^6 \quad \underset{\text{of N}}{\text{IV}} \quad \text{V} \quad \text{I} \qquad \text{I} \longrightarrow \text{Em} \qquad \text{I}^6$$

$$\text{I} \qquad\qquad\qquad\qquad\qquad\qquad \text{V} \qquad \text{I}$$

b

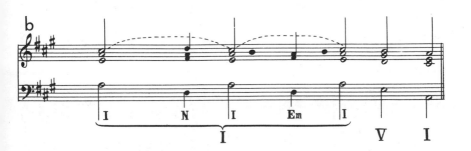

$$\text{I} \qquad \text{N} \qquad \text{I} \qquad \text{Em} \qquad \text{I}$$

$$\text{I} \qquad\qquad\qquad\qquad\qquad \text{V} \qquad \text{I}$$

314

a

$$\text{I} \qquad\quad \text{N} \qquad\quad \text{II}^6 \;\; \text{V} \qquad \text{I}$$

b

$$\text{I} \qquad \underset{\text{of P}}{\text{II}^6 \;\; \text{V} \;\; \text{I}} \qquad \text{II}^6 \;\; \text{V} \qquad \text{I}$$

315 CHOPIN Mazurka, Op 68, No. 2 (Posth.)

316 SCHUBERT German Dance, No. 7

316 cont'd

317

318 HAYDN Piano Sonata, G minor, No. 44

319 PURCELL Overture, "Dido and Aeneas"

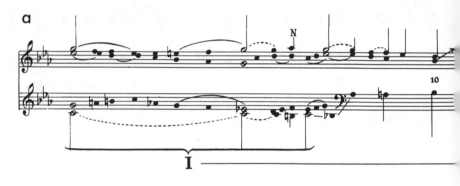

320 PEERSON The Primerose

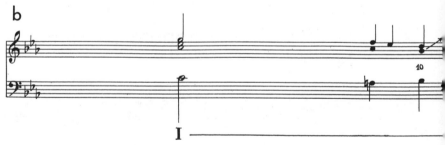

321 BACH Chorale (No. 229)

a

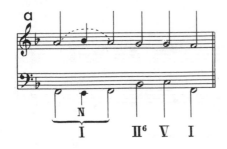

I   V   I⁶

I

CS   I   II⁶₅   V   I

322

a

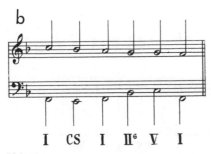

N

I   II⁶   V   I

b

I   CS   I   II⁶   V   I

323   COUPERIN La Bandoline

a

I   CS   I⁶
          (CS)

II⁶   V   I

324   CHOPIN Nocturne, Op 9, No. 2

Andante

espress. dolce

324 cont'd

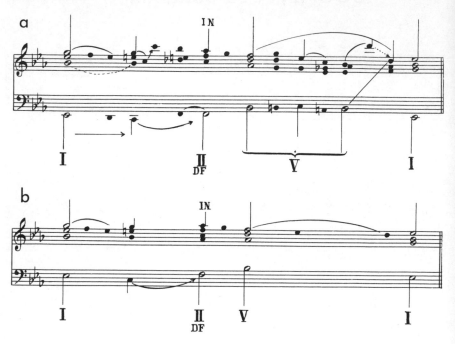

325 SCHUMANN Piano Concerto

325 cont'd

326

327   BACH Chorale (No. 320)

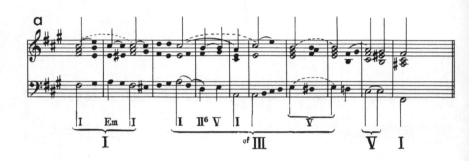

I   Em   I   I   II⁶ V   I   V̆

I   ᵒᶠ III   V̆   I

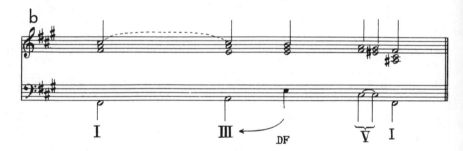

I   III ← DF   V̆   I

328   BACH Chorale (No. 280)

I   IV   ⁽ᴵᴵ⁾ DF   V̆   I

329   HANDEL Courante (Suite No. 14)

SCHUBERT Impromptu, Op 90, No. 2

331 VAUGHAN-WILLIAMS
Symphony No. 5

[P. 8, SCORE]

332 MOZART Rondo, K. 494

332 cont'd

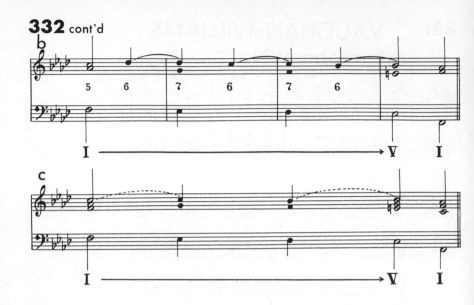

333 SCHUBERT Waltz Op 77, No. 10

334 SCHUBERT Täuschung

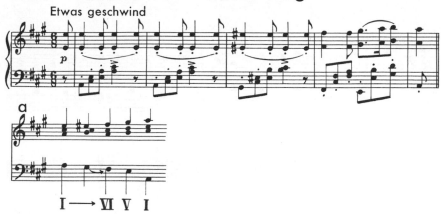

335 WEBER Overture, "Der Freischütz"

336 HAYDN String Quartet, Op 76, No. 4

337 SCHUBERT Piano Sonata, B♭ Major

338

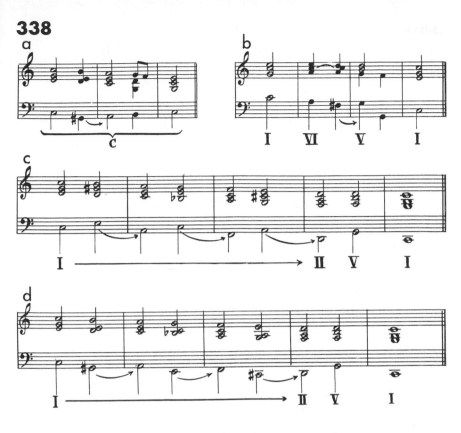

339   BACH Chorale (No. 361)

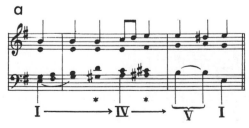

340

341

342

343

344

345

346

129

347 BACH Chorale (No. 166)

I   II$^6_5$ ⟶ V   I

348 BACH Chorale (No. 167)

I ⟶ IV ⟶ V I

349 HAYDN String Quartet, Op 76, No. 1

Adagio sostenuto

a

I   V

N ⟶ N

b

N   N

I   V

350 CHOPIN Mazurka, Op 24, No. 3

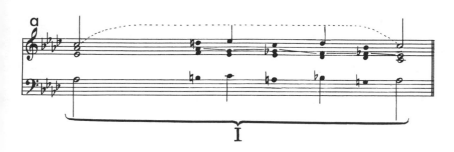

I

351 WOLF Schlafendes Jesuskind

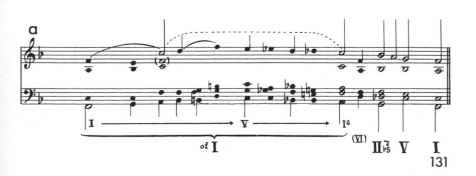

352

353

354

a

I II⁶ V I

b

I   P   II⁶ V   I

c

I ⟶ P   II⁶ V   I

355

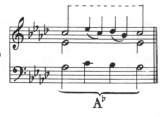

from

A♭   A♭

356

C

358 SCHUMANN Novelette, Op 21, No. 2

Ausserst rasch und mit Bravour

a
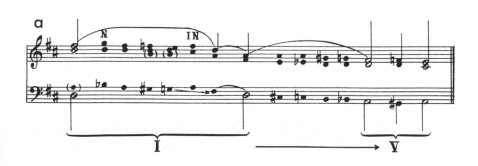

b
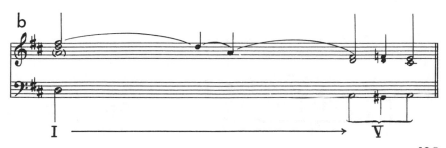

359 CHOPIN Mazurka, Op 17, No. 4

Lento, ma non troppo

a

b

I

I

360 WAGNER Siegfried's Rhine Journey ("Götterdämmerung")

Rasch

f vigoroso

a

F

CHOPIN Mazurka, Op 7, No. 2

362   CHOPIN Mazurka, Op 6, No. 1

a

b

c

d

e

363   SCHUMANN Novelette, Op 21, No. 8

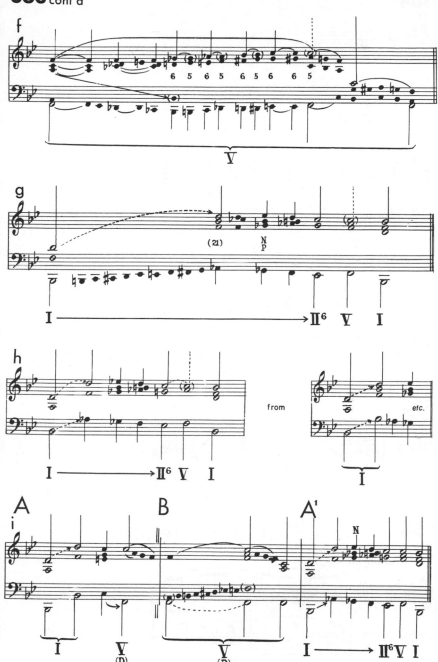

364

365

becomes

366   SCHUBERT Tränenregen

Ziemlich langsam

I   II   V

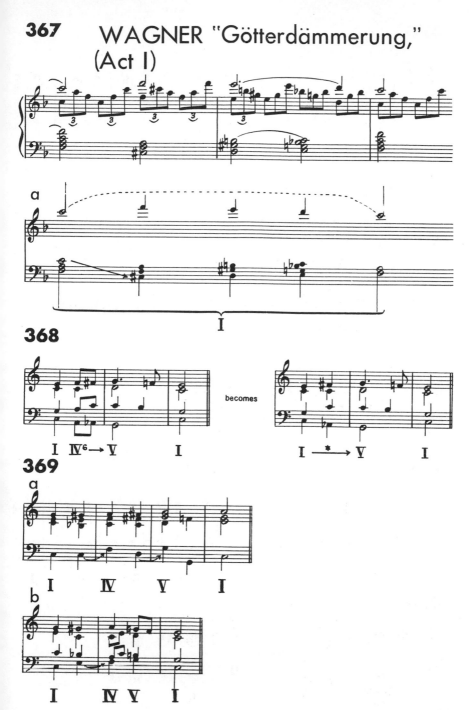

367 WAGNER "Götterdämmerung," (Act I)

368

becomes

I IV⁶→ V   I

I →* V   I

369

a
I   IV   V   I

b
I   IV V   I

370

a

I   *   V   I

b

I   *   V   I

c

I   VI   *   V   I

371   WAGNER Prelude, "Tristan und Isolde"

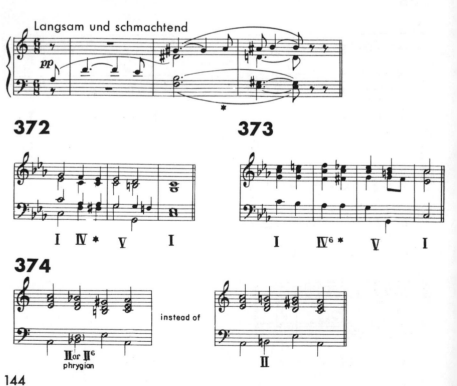

Langsam und schmachtend

pp

*

372

I   IV *   V   I

373

I   IV⁶ *   V   I

374

II or II⁶
phrygian

instead of

II

375 BEETHOVEN Piano Sonata,
C# minor, Op 27, No. 2

376 WEBER "Der Freischütz" (Act II,
No. 6)

R. STRAUSS "Ariadne auf Naxos"

Mezzo movimento

[P. 216, PIANO-VOCAL SCORE]

378 CHOPIN Nocturne, Op 27, No. 1

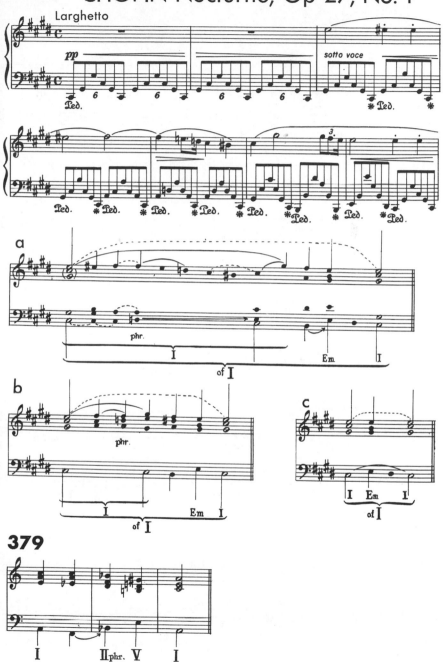

379

147

380 PROKOFIEFF Gavotte, Op 77, No. 4

Allegro moderato

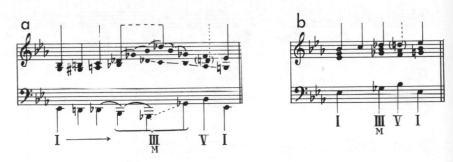

381 R. STRAUSS Don Juan

Allegro molto con brio

382 **WOLF In dem Schatten meiner Locken**

Leicht, zart, nicht schnell

In dem Schat-ten mei-ner Lo-cken schlief mir mein Ge-lieb-ter

molto rit.

ein. Weck' ich ihn nun auf?

Ach nein!

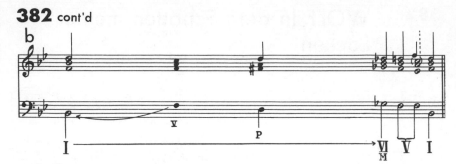

383 # BEETHOVEN Piano Sonata, C minor, Op 13

Adagio cantabile

a

b

384 SCHUBERT Piano Sonata,
C minor

384 cont'd

a

I —————————————→ VI V I
                M

b

5 6 8   5 6 8

+   −
I ———————————————→ VI V I
  M   M

c

I♭ VI V I♮

385 SCHUBERT Pause

Ziemlich geschwind

(46)

Nun lie-be Lau-te, ruh' an dem Na-gel. hier,   und weht ein

152

385 cont'd

Lüft - chen ü - ber die Sai - ten __ dir, und streift ei - ne Bie - ne mit

ih - ren Flü-geln dich, da wird mir so ban - ge, und es durchschauert mich.

War-um liess ich das Band auch hän-gen so lang? Oft

fliegt's um die Sai - ten mit seuf-zen-dem Klang. Ist es der Nach-klang

385 cont'd

mei-ner Lie - bes - pein? Soll es das Vor - spiel_ neu- er Lie - der sein?

a

I ⟶ II ⟶ V I
(DF)

double mixture

b

I ⟶ II ⟶ V I

386 MAHLER Das Lied von der Erde, No. 6

Langsam

Ich — su - che Ru - he, Ru - he für_ mein_ ein - - - - sam Herz!

espress.

386 cont'd

a

387 CHOPIN Mazurka, Op 68, No. 4 (Posth.)

155

387 cont'd

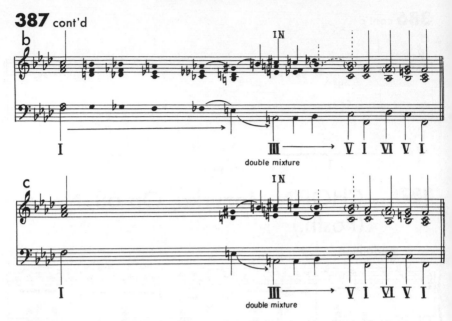

388 MOZART Piano Sonata, F Major, K. 280

SCHUBERT Trio, B♭ Major, Op 99

HAYDN Piano Sonata, F Major, No. 29

391 SCHUMANN Forest Scenes, No. 6

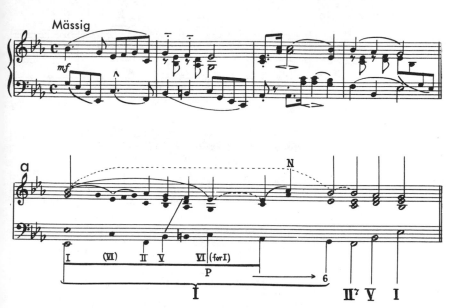

392 BACH Chorale (No. 5)

393 CHOPIN Waltz, Op 64, No. 2

160

394 SCHUBERT Piano Sonata, B♭ Major

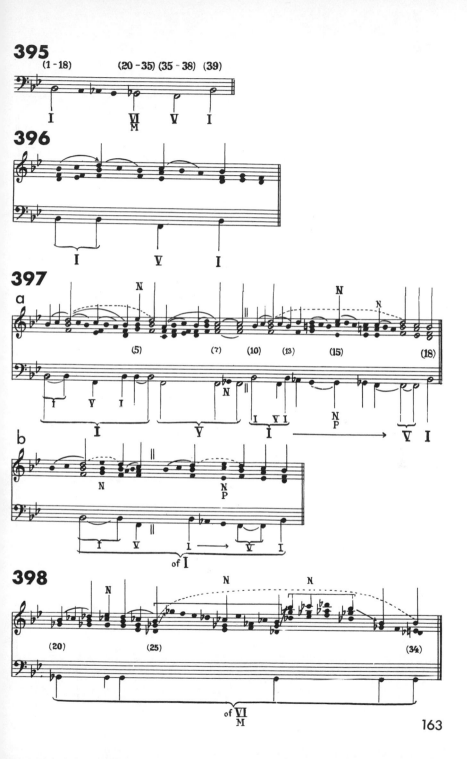

163

399

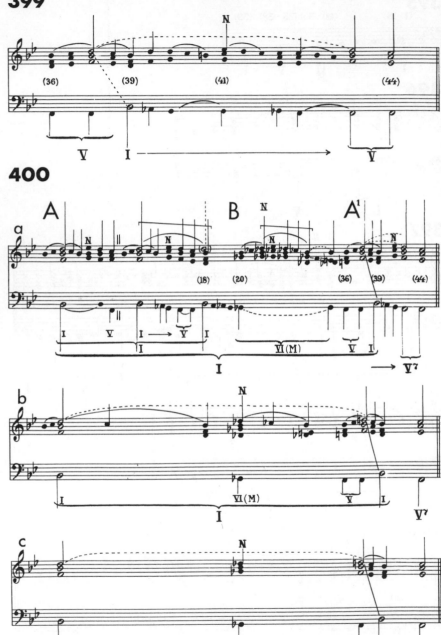

400

401   HAYDN String Quartet, Op 20, No. 5

LASSO Motet: Recordare Jesu pie

e, quod sum cau - sa tu-ae vi - - -ae ne

quod sum cau - - - -sa tu - ae vi - - ae ne me

sum cau - - - - - - - - sa tu - - ae vi - - - - - - - -ae

_ sum cau - sa, quod sum cau - - - - sa tu - - -ae vi - - - ae

_ sum _ cau - - - sa tu - ae vi - - - - - -ae

quod sum cau - - - - sa tu - - ae vi - - ae

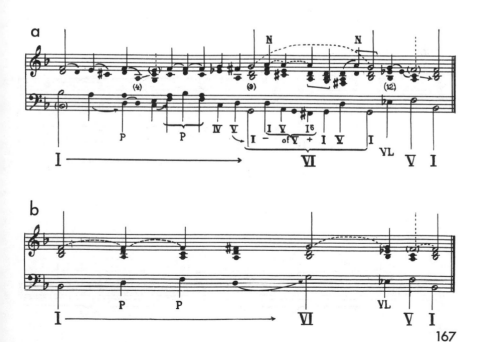

a

b

403   GASTOLDI Balletto: Speme amorosa

[From SHM, No. 20]

a

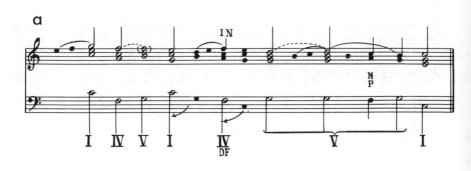

b

(1-4)   (5-8)

404 WAGNER "Tristan und Isolde"
(Act II)

Nun führst du in dein Ei - - gen, dein Er - - be mir zu zei - - gen; wie flöh' ich wohl das Land, das al - le Welt um-spannt?

169

FRANCK Prelude, Aria and Finale

Allegro moderato e maestoso

a

b

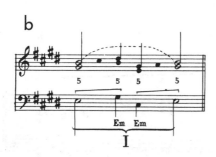

cont'd

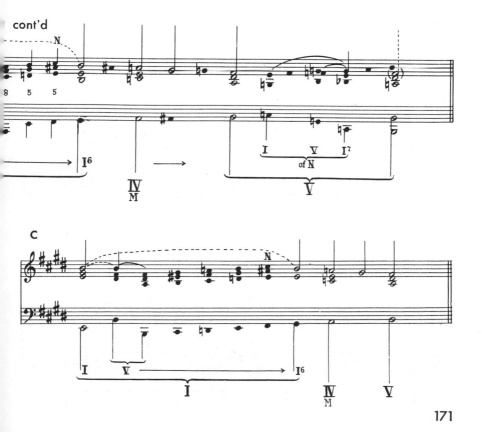

406 R. STRAUSS Quintet ("Ariadne auf Naxos")

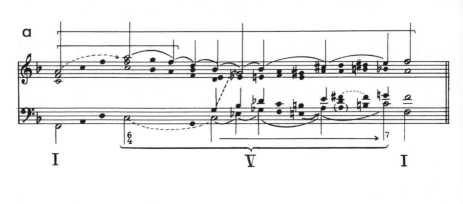

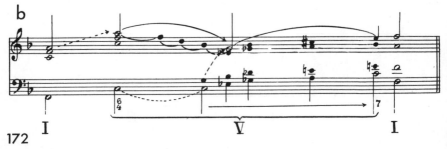

172

407 R. STRAUSS Quintet ("Ariadne auf Naxos")

Poco tranquillo

a

I ⟶ III V I
　　　　　M

b

I ⟶ III V I
　　　　　M

408 BIZET Seguidilla ("Carmen," Act I)

Allegretto

Près des rem - parts de Sé - vil - - - - - le,

408 cont'd

Chez ___ mon a - mi ___ Lil - las Pas - tia ___ J'i-

rai dan - ser la Sé - gue - dille Et boi - re du Man - za - nil - la ___

J'i - rai chez mon a - mi Lil-las Pas - tia. ___

409 CHOPIN Polonaise-Fantasy

a

174

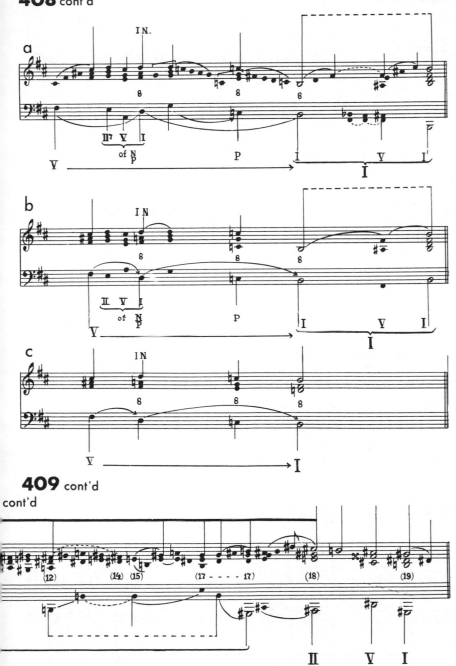

409 cont'd

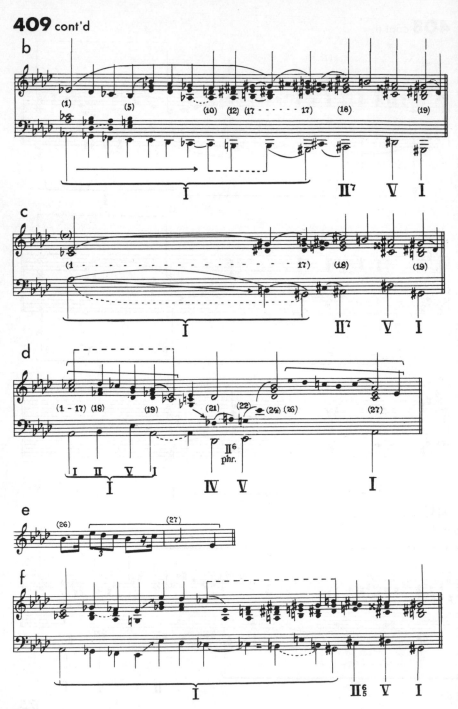

176

410 HINDEMITH Piano Sonata No. 2.

a

b

c

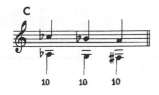

411 MARTINŮ Sonata for Cello and Piano No. 2.

412 COPLAND 3 Excerpts from "Our Town," No. 1

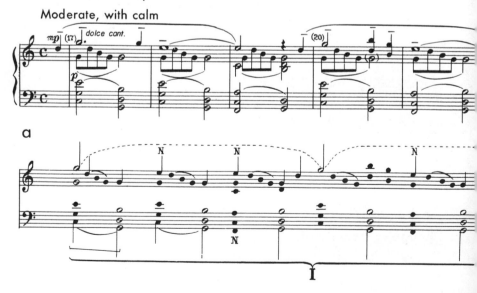

413 WAGENAAR Ciacona

Adagio

a

b   c

D

414 MARTINŮ Sonata for Violin and Piano No. 2

Larghetto

a

$B^b \; {}^6_4$

415 RAVEL Jeux d'eau

415 cont'd

a

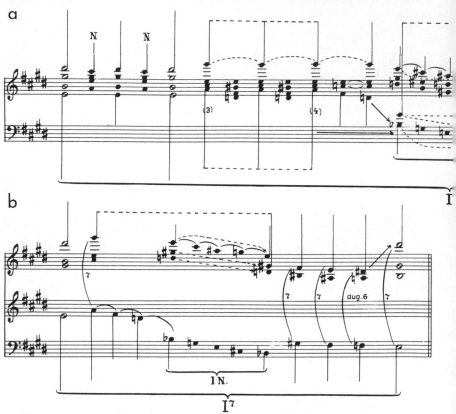

b

416 COPLAND Piano Sonata

Molto moderato

cont'd

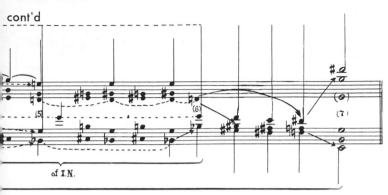

of I.N.

c

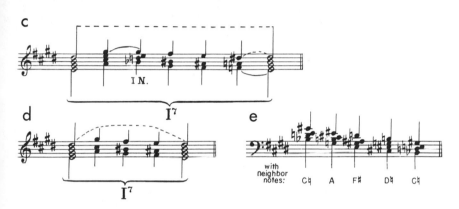

I N.

d

I^7

e

with
neighbor
notes: C♮   A   F♯   D♮   C♮

I^7

(200)

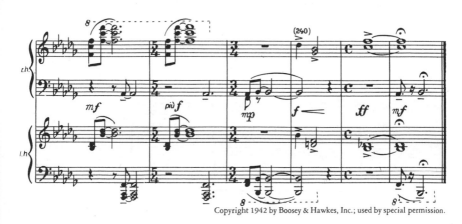

a

a cont'd

a cont'd

c

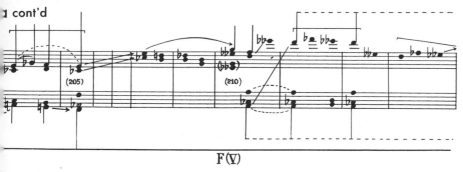

1 cont'd

(205)   (210)

F (V̱)

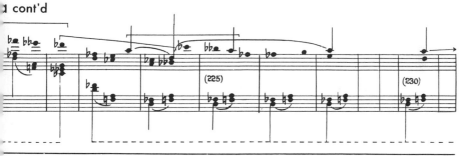

1 cont'd

(225)   (230)

F (V̱)

b

(197)   (205)   (210)   (214)   (216) (223)   (237)

F (V̱)
polychord

d

(197-237)

417 STRAVINSKY Symphony in Three Movements

a

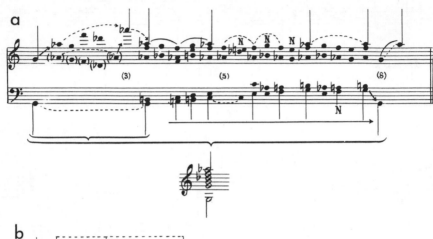

b

418 BARTOK Bagatelle Op 6, No. 4

419 R. STRAUSS "Elektra"

420   BEETHOVEN Piano Concerto
No. 4, G Major

a

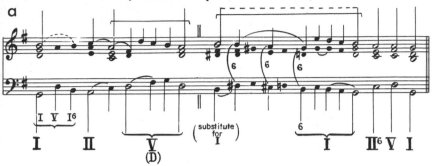

I   II   V   (substitute for I)   I   II⁶ V I
(D)

421

a

b

c

422

a

b

423

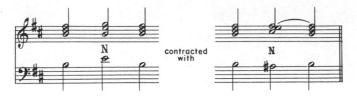

424 BACH Cantata: Du wahrer Gott und Davids Sohn

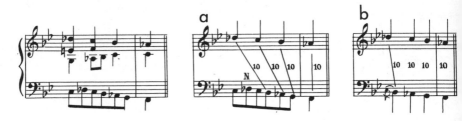

425 SCHUMANN Romance, Op 28, No. 1

426   COUPERIN La Favorite

a

b

427   BYRD Sacerdotes Domini

a

428 MOUSSORGSKY Ballet of the Unhatched Chickens (Pictures from an Exhibition)

429 VERDI Oro supplex (Requiem)

430 BEETHOVEN Piano Sonata, C Major, Op 53. Introduzione

431 CHOPIN Polonaise, Op 26

431 cont'd

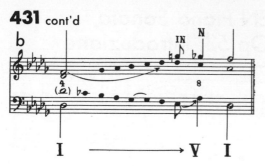

I ⟶ V I

432

a

CHOPIN Mazurka, Op 59, No. 2

I

b

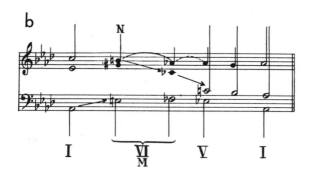

I VI̲/M V I

431 cont'd

c

IN   N

I   V   I

d

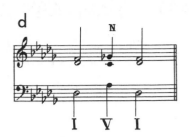

N

I   V   I

432 cont'd

cont'd

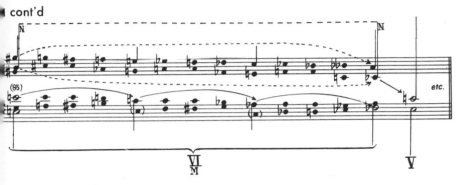

N   N

(85)   etc.

$$\frac{\text{VI}}{\text{M}}$$ V

433   CHOPIN Polonaise, Op 40

a

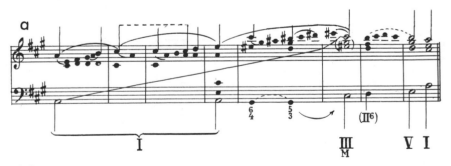

$^6_4$ $^5_3$ (II^6)

I $\frac{\text{III}}{\text{M}}$ V   I

434

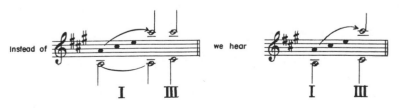

Instead of   we hear

I   III   I   III

435 FARNABY A Toye

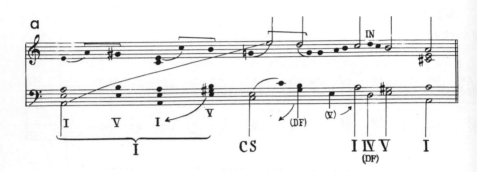

436 MENDELSSOHN Overture,
"A Midsummer Night's Dream"

Allegro di molto

437 SCHUBERT Piano Sonata, C minor

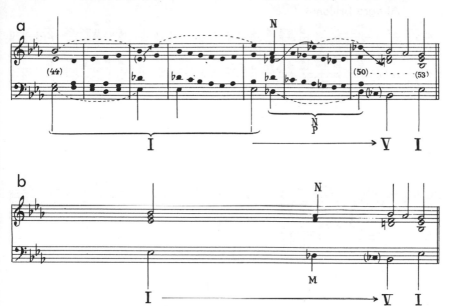

438 SCHUBERT Fantasia-Sonata

439   SCHUMANN Piano Quintet

Allegro brillante

a

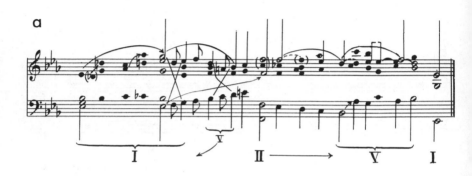

I   V   II ———→   V   I

441   BARTÓK From 10 Easy Pieces for Piano

Poco andante

a

(I)   IV⁶   V I   IV⁶

of I   M   of III

439 cont'd

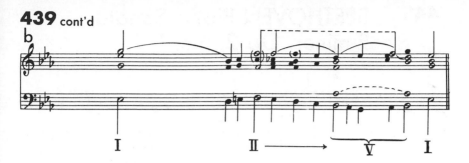

b

I   II ⟶ V   I

440 BEETHOVEN Piano Sonata, G Major, Op 31, No. 1

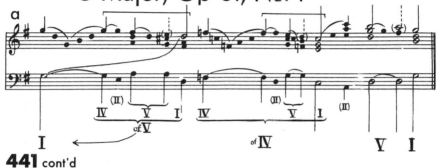

a

IV (II) V I IV (II) V I (II)
       of V

I ⟵   of IV   V   I

441 cont'd

pp   mp   poco sf   dim.   p   pp

a cont'd

V I   ⟶ V I

442 BEETHOVEN Piano Sonata, F minor, Op 2, No. 1

a

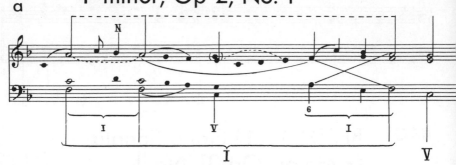

443 BEETHOVEN Piano Sonata, C minor, Op 10, No. 1.

a

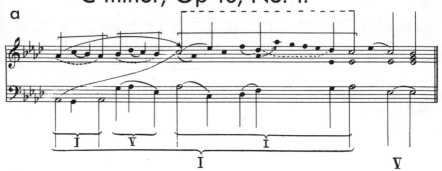

444 MOZART Piano Sonata, C Major, K. 279

a

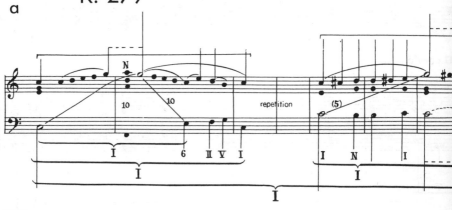

442 cont'd

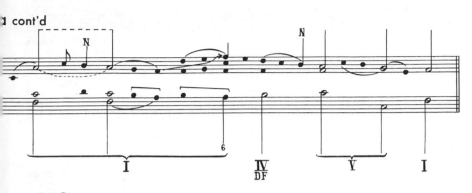

443 cont'd

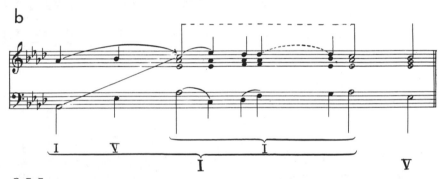

444 cont'd

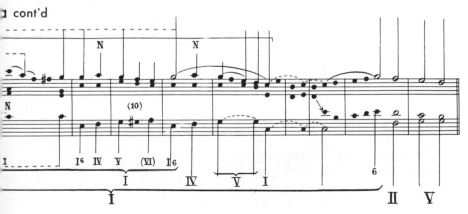

Nun will die

Sonn' so hell auf - geh'n, als sei kein

a

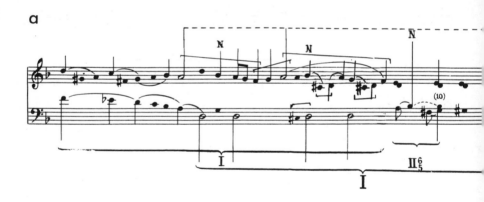

446

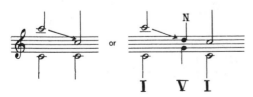

or

I V I

445 cont'd

Un - glück, kein _ Un - glück ___ die _ Nacht ___ ge - scheh'n! __

a cont'd

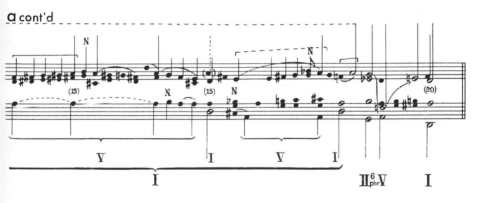

447 ALLEMANDE

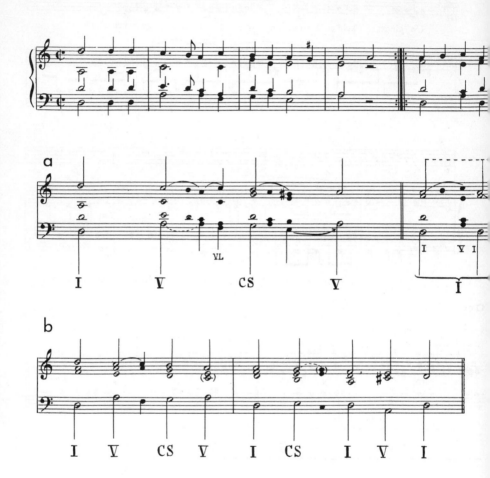

447 cont'd

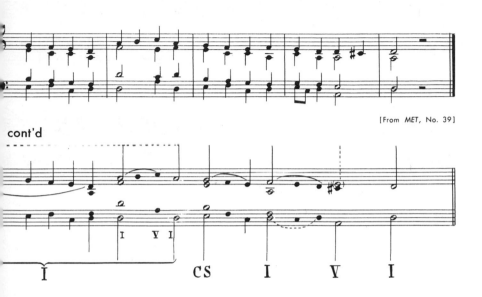

[From *MET*, No. 39]

cont'd

I V I

I   CS   I   V   I

448   SCHUBERT Die Krähe

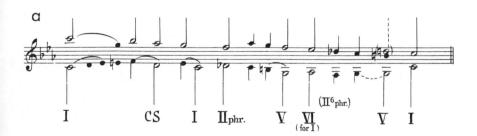

a

I   CS   I $II_{phr.}$ V $\underset{(\text{for } I)}{VI}$ V   I

$(II^6_{phr.})$

449 RAMEAU Choeur des Spartiates ("Castor et Pollux," Act I)

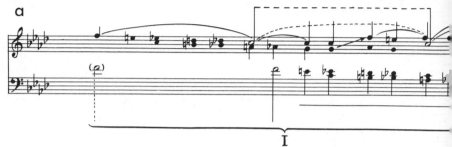

450 BEETHOVEN Piano Sonata, E minor, Op 90

449 cont'd

450 cont'd

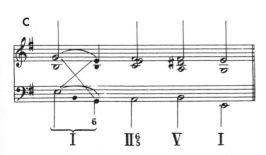

PROKOFIEFF Piano Sonata No. 8, Op 84

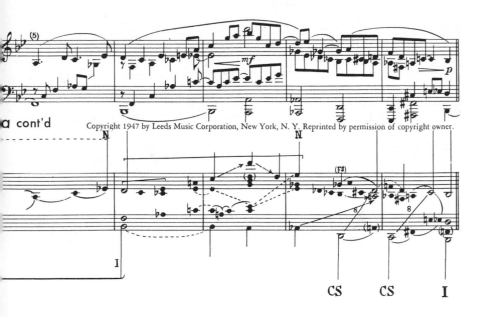

a cont'd

452 BARTÓK String Quartet No. 5

Adagio molto

Un poco più Andante

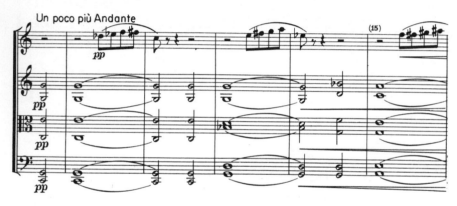

a

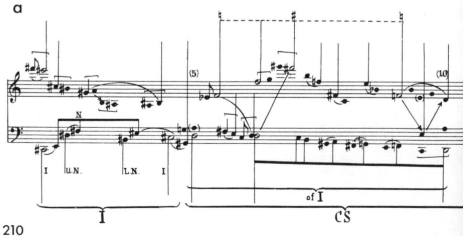

452 cont'd

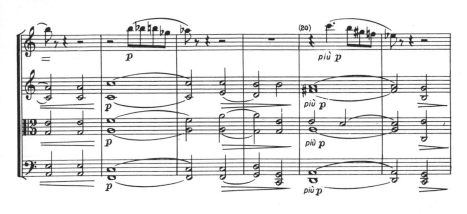

cont'd

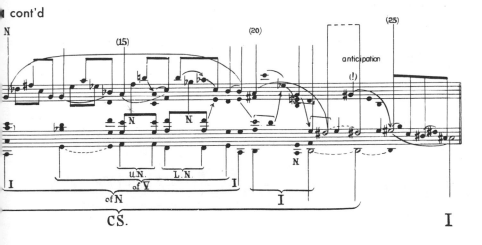

452 cont'd

b

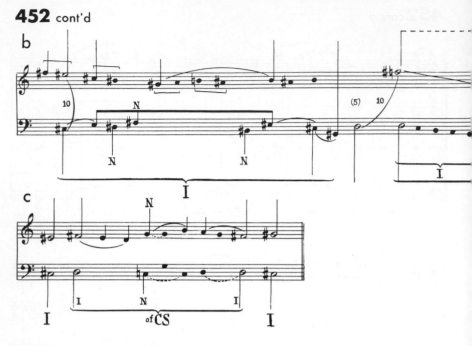

c

453 HINDEMITH Piano Sonata No. 1

With quiet motion, in quarters

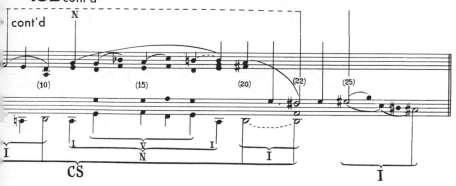

453 cont'd

453 cont'd

a

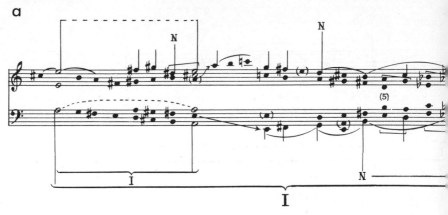

a cont'd

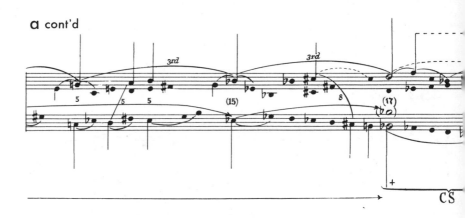

b

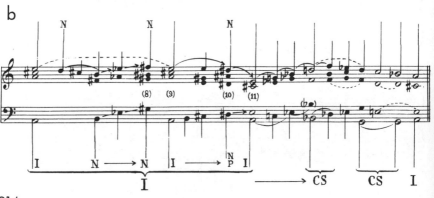

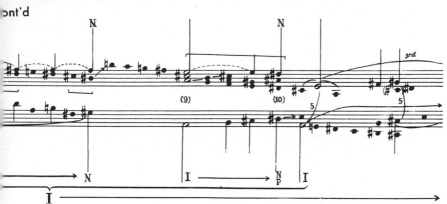

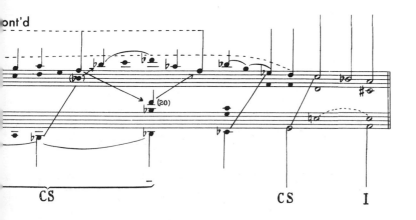

ont'd

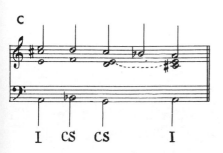

a

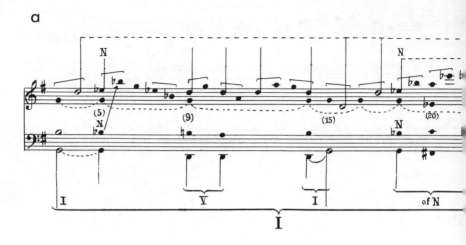

a cont'd

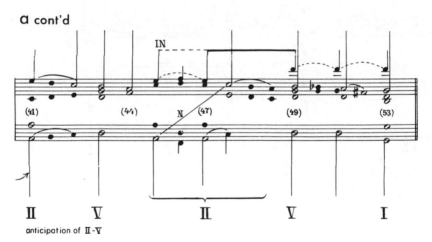

anticipation of II-V

nt'd

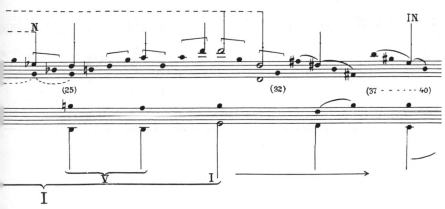

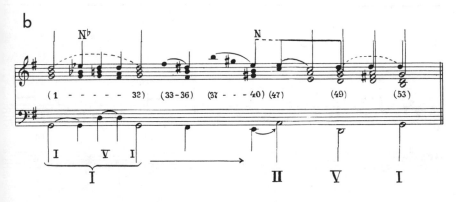

455 DEBUSSY Prélude à l'après-midi d'un faune

a

b

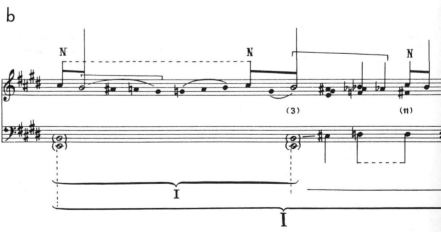

456 CHOPIN Nocturne, Op 48, No. 2

a

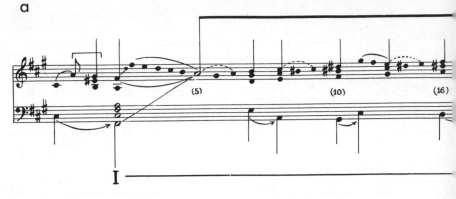

b

457 PROKOFIEFF Piano Sonata No. 3

a

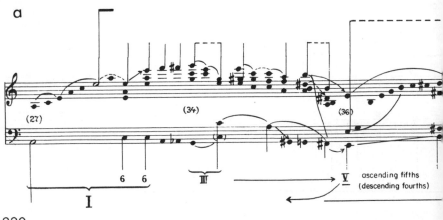

456 cont'd

cont'd

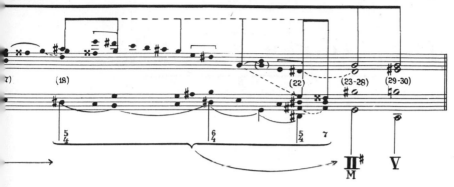

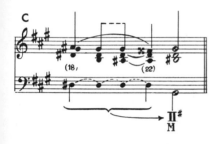

457 cont'd

cont'd

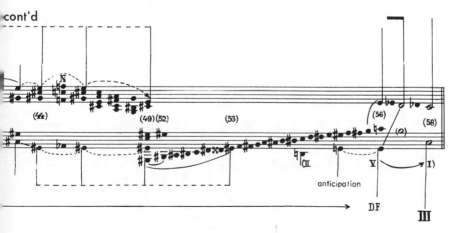

221

457 cont'd

b

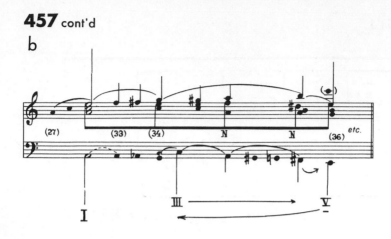

d

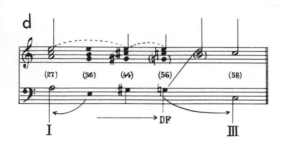

458 BEETHOVEN Piano Sonata,
D Major, Op 10, No. 3

a

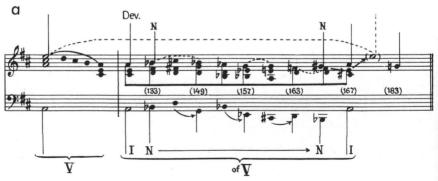

457 cont'd

c

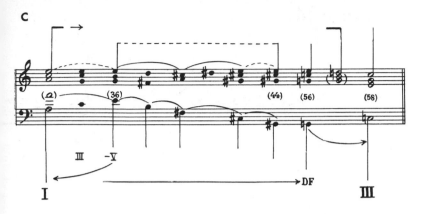

458 cont'd

b

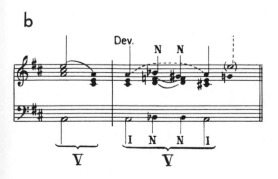

459 HAYDN Symphony D Major, No. 104

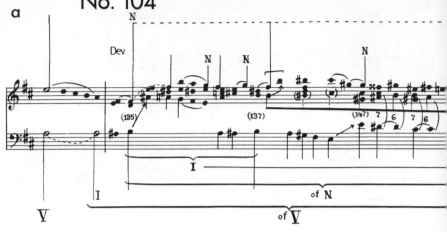

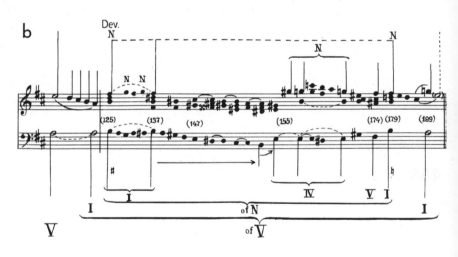

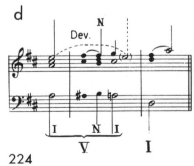

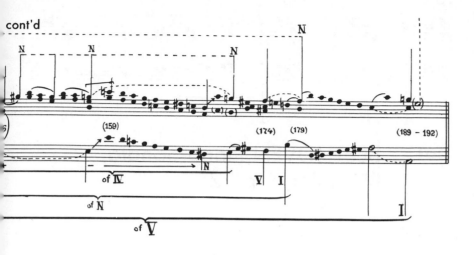

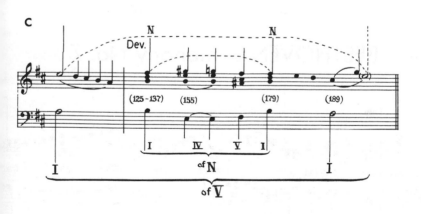

460

461 BEETHOVEN Piano Sonata, Bᵇ Major, Op 22

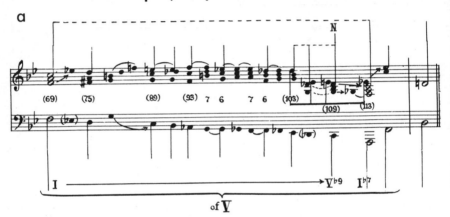

462 BEETHOVEN Symphony No. 7

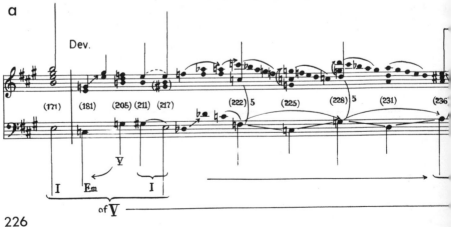

460 cont'd

C

461 cont'd

b   c

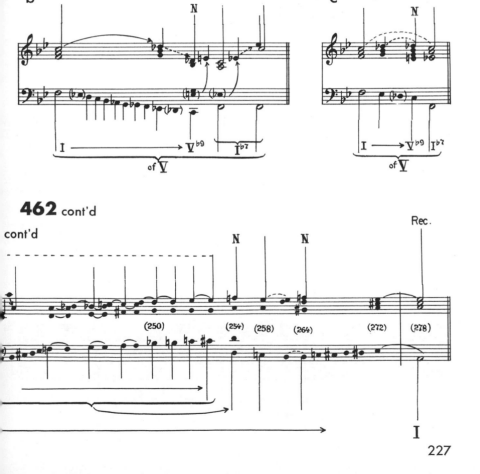

462 cont'd

cont'd

Rec.

227

462 cont'd

b

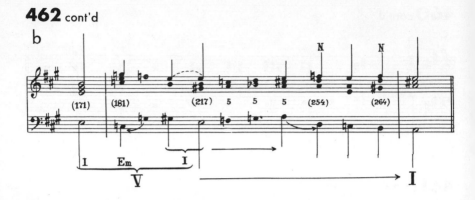

463 BEETHOVEN Piano Sonata,
C minor, Op 10, No. 1

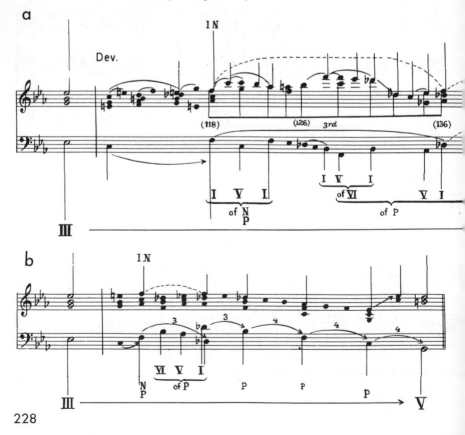

462 cont'd

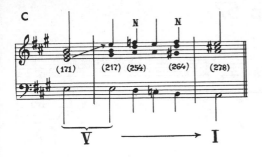

463 cont'd

cont'd

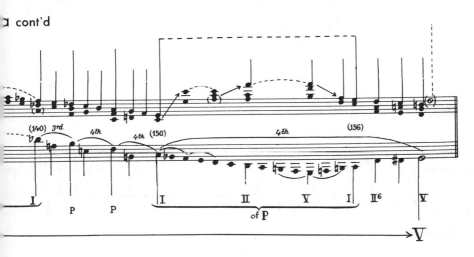

464   BEETHOVEN Piano Sonata,
F minor, Op 57

a

b

c

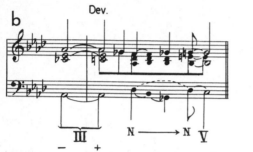

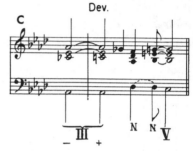

465

a   b

466

a   b

c   d

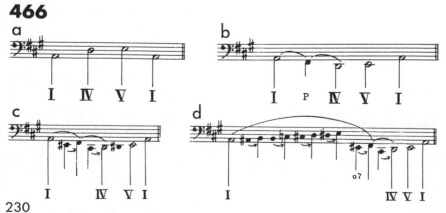

470 cont'd

c

I   IV   V   I

471   WAGNER "Parsifal," (Act I)

a

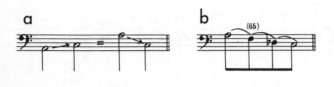

b

c

d

e

g cont'd

471 cont'd

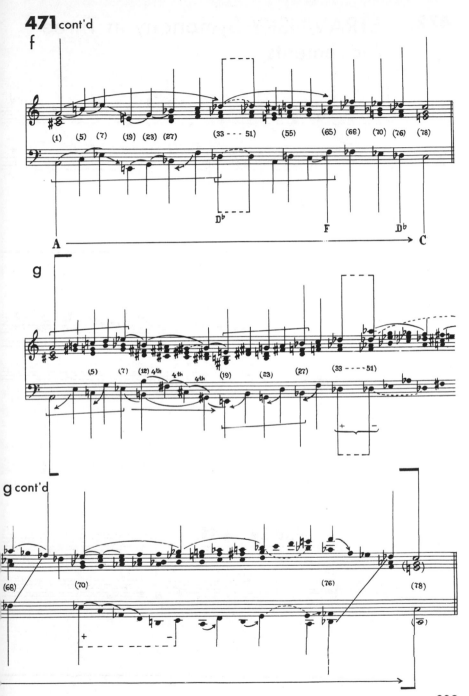

STRAVINSKY Symphony in Three
Movements

472 cont'd

b

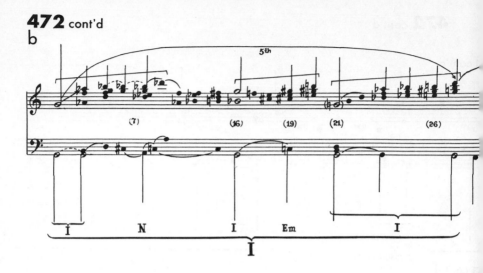

c

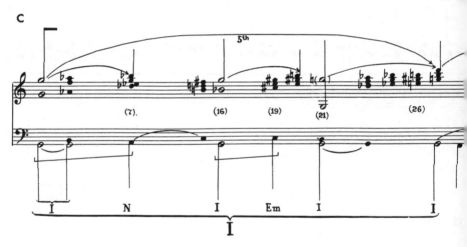

d

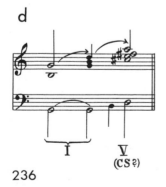

236

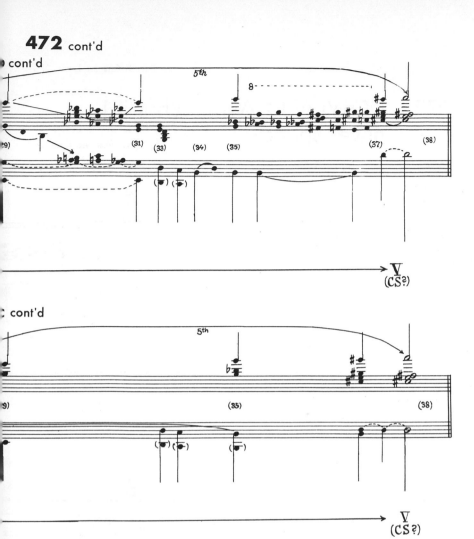

473 DOWLAND Ayre: What if I never speed

[From *HAM*, Vol. I, No. 163]

a

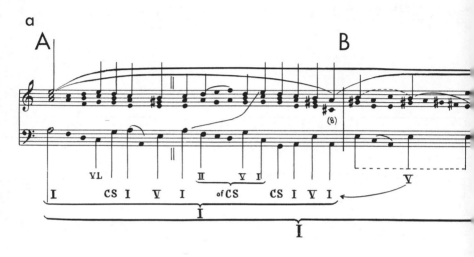

b

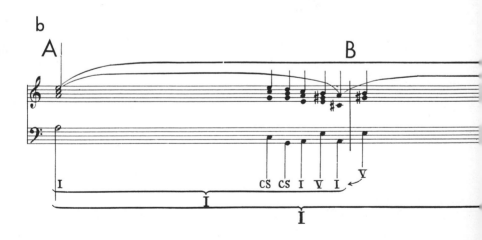

cont'd

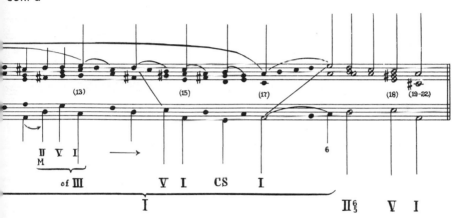

cont'd

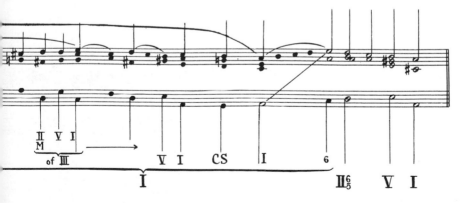

BACH Fugue No. 5 (Well-Tempered Clavier, Bk I)

a

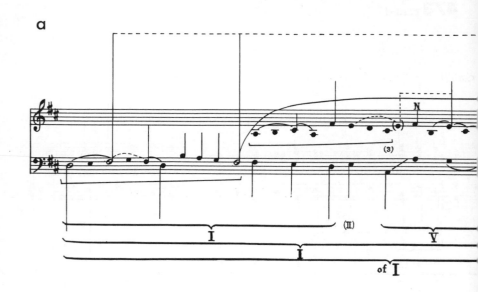

a cont'd

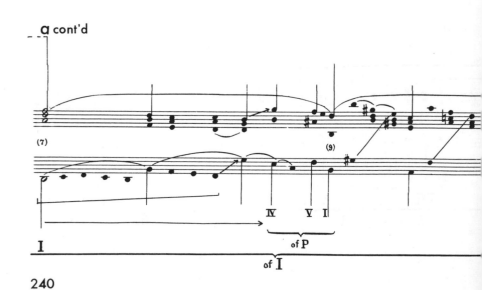

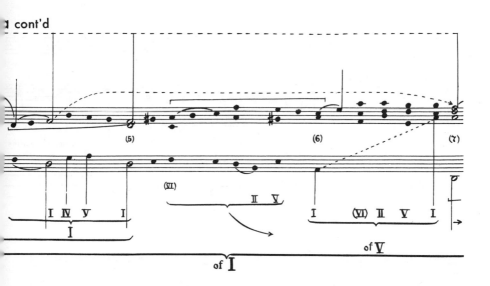

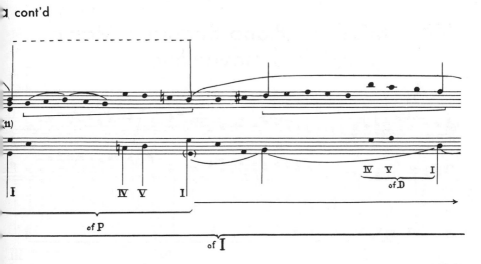

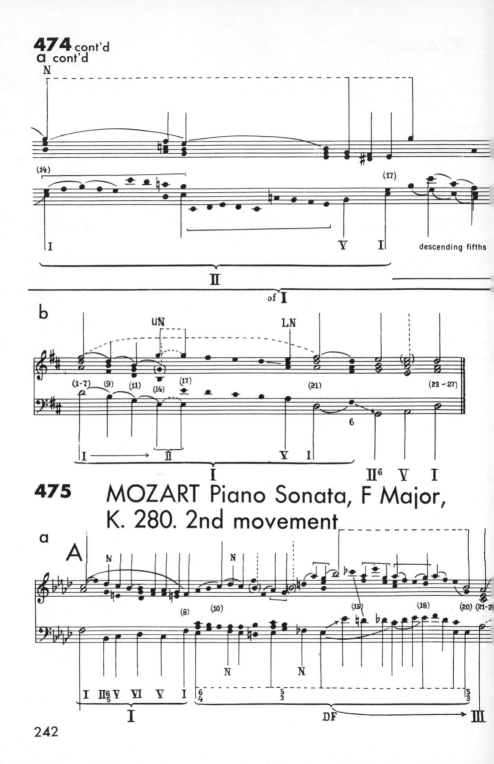

474 cont'd
a cont'd

descending fifths

475 MOZART Piano Sonata, F Major, K. 280. 2nd movement

242

a cont'd

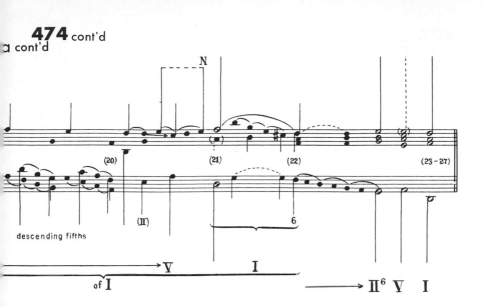

a cont'd

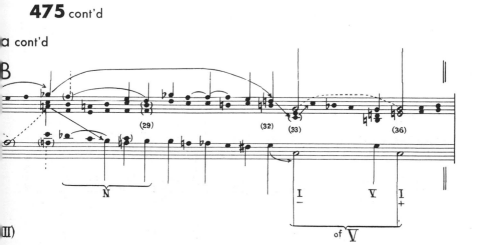

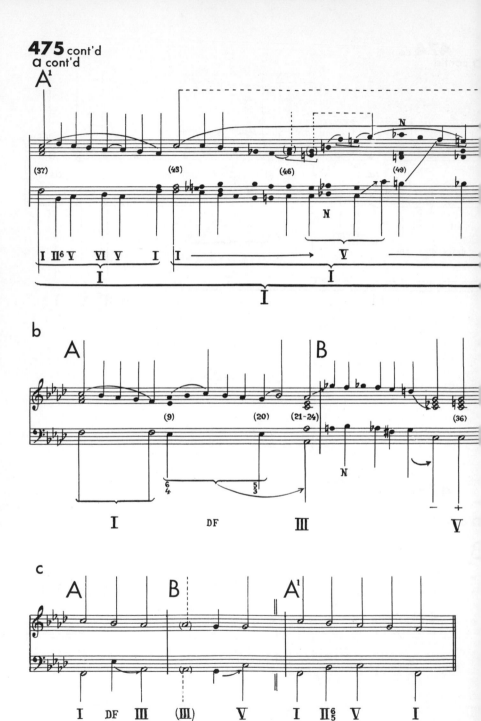

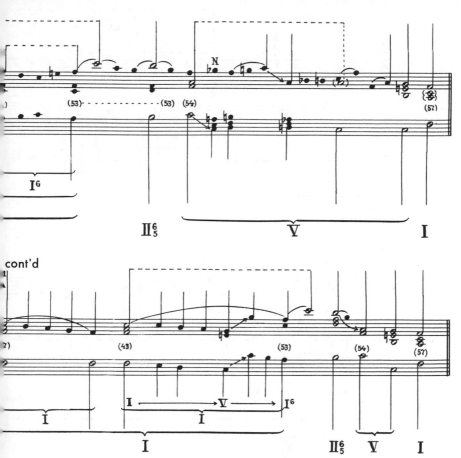

477 BRAHMS Intermezzo, Op. 119, No. 1

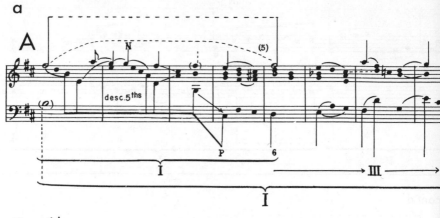

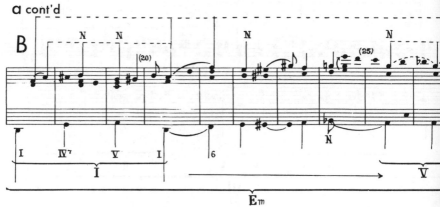

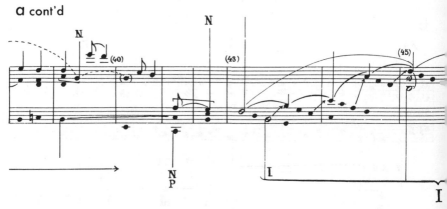

cont'd

cont'd

cont'd

a cont'd

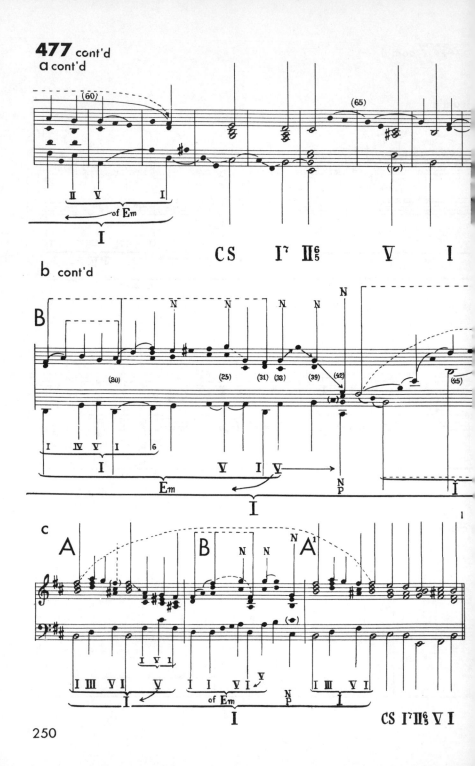

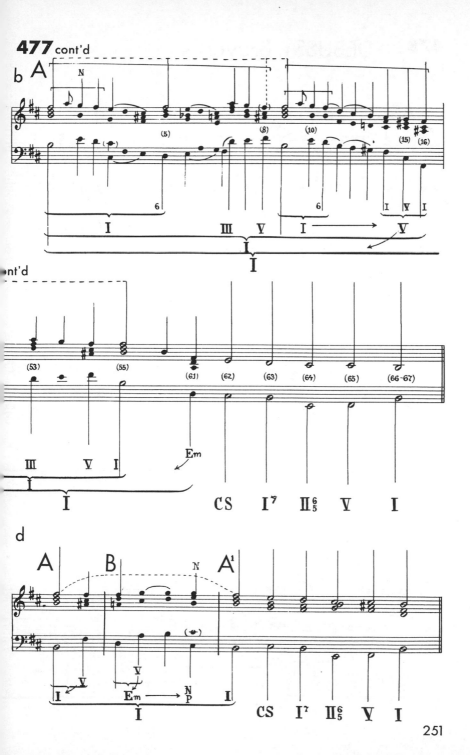

a

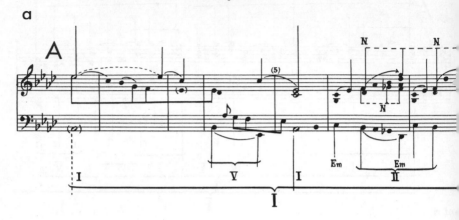

a cont'd

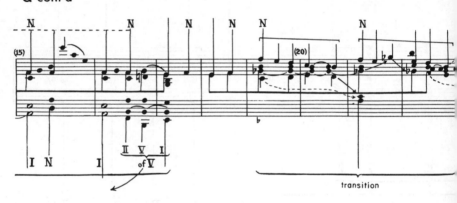

a cont'd

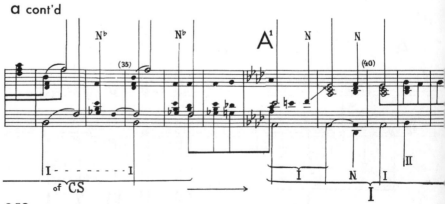

cont'd

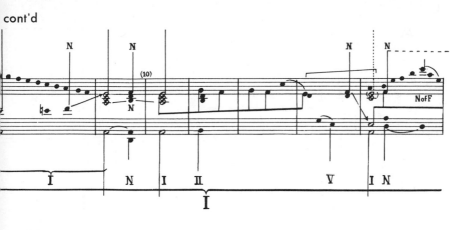

cont'd

B

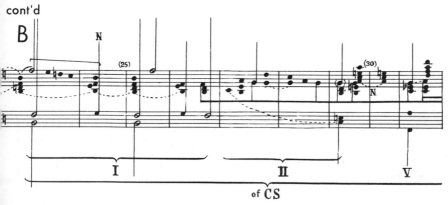

cont'd

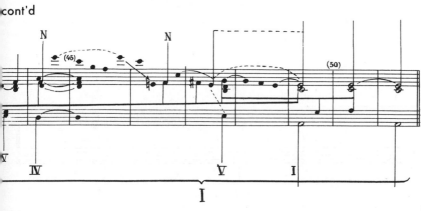

478 cont'd

b

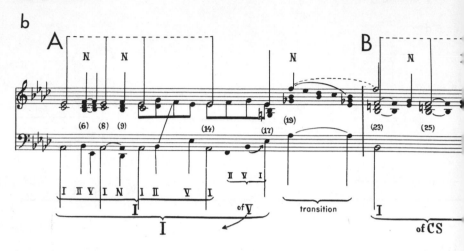

c

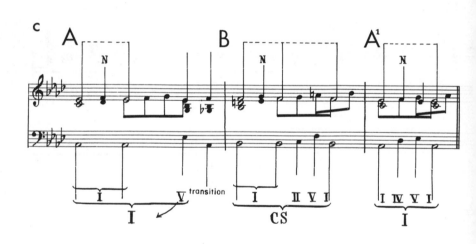

d

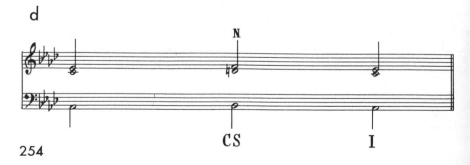

254

b cont'd

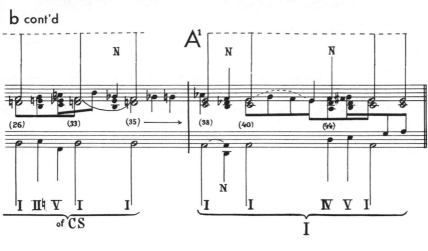

e

Melodic prolongations:

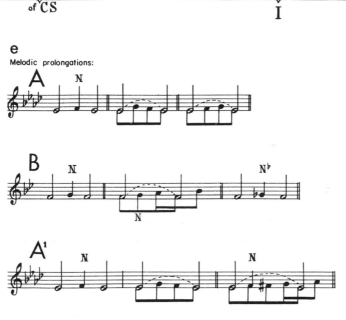

479 GESUALDO Madrigal: Io pur respiro

[From *HAM*, Vol. I, No. 161]

BARTÓK Piano Concerto No. 3.
1st movement

a

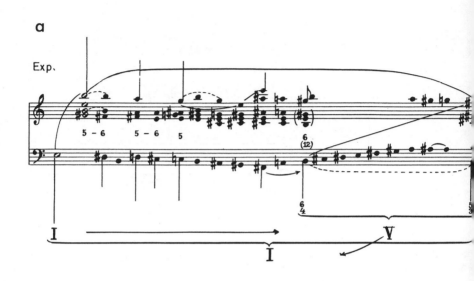

a cont'd

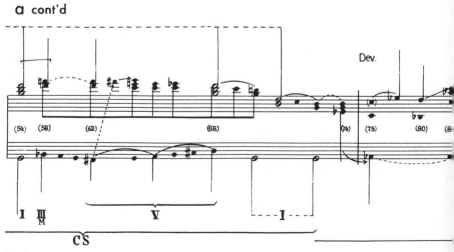

cont'd

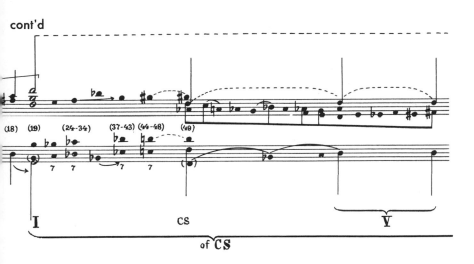

(18) (19) (24-34) (37-43) (44-48) (49)

I   CS   V

of CS

 cont'd

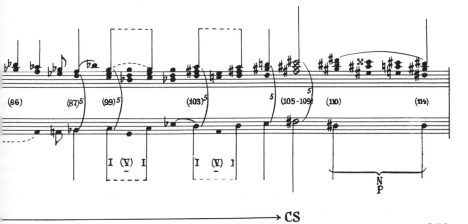

(86) (87)⁵ (99)⁵ (103)⁵ ⁵ (105-109) (110) (114)

I (V) I   I (V) I   N P

⟶ CS

ɑ cont'd

Rec.

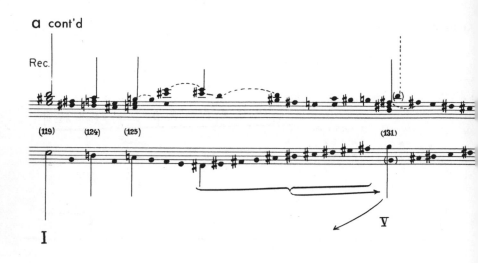

(119)   (124)   (125)   (131)

I   V

ɑ cont'd

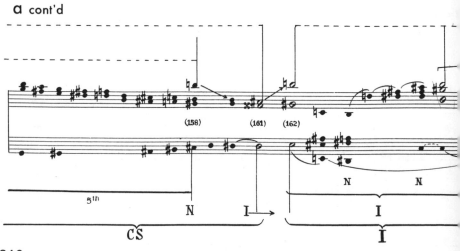

(158)   (161)   (162)

5th   N   N

N   I   I

CS   I

a cont'd

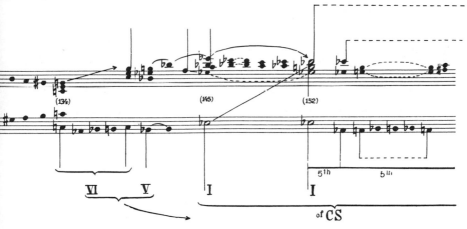

a cont'd

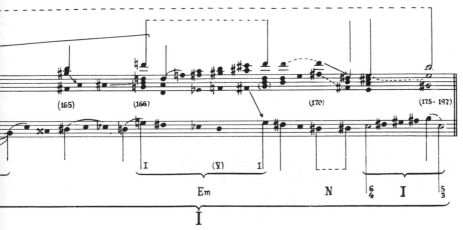

b

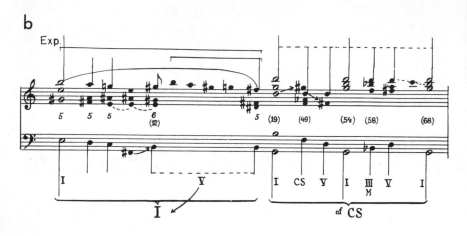

b cont'd

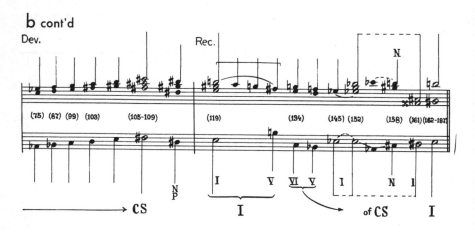

c

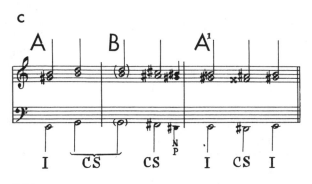

481

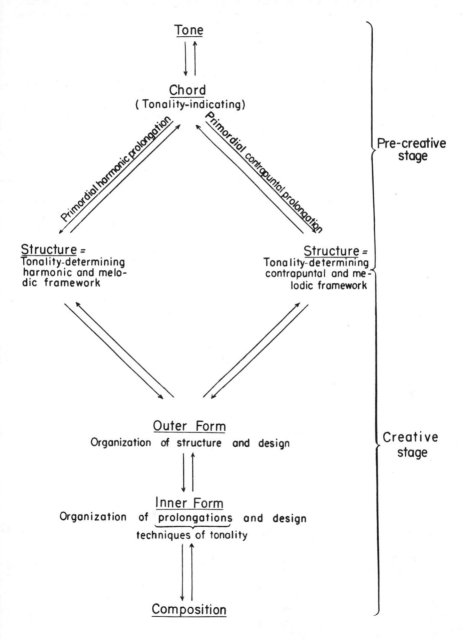

Tone

Chord
(Tonality-indicating)

Primordial harmonic prolongation

Primordial contrapuntal prolongation

Pre-creative
stage

Structure =
Tonality-determining
harmonic and melo-
dic framework

Structure =
Tonality-determining
contrapuntal and me-
lodic framework

Outer Form
Organization of structure and design

Inner Form
Organization of prolongations and design
techniques of tonality

Composition

Creative
stage

MARENZIO Madrigal: Io piango

[From *SHM*, No. 18]

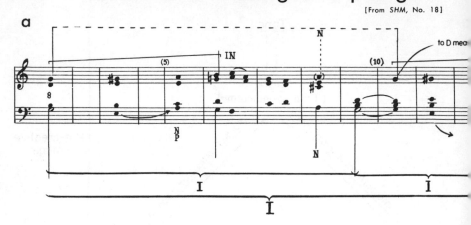

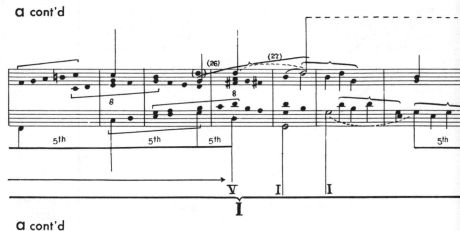

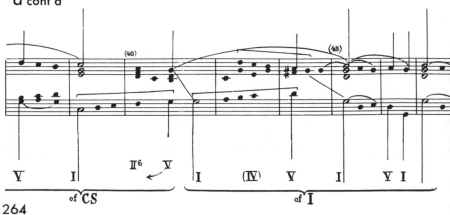

482 cont'd

b

483 MOZART Aria ("The Magic Flute")

a

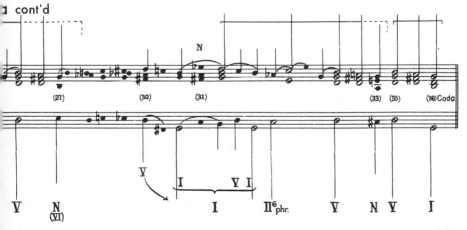

484 FRESCOBALDI Corrente

[From AMI, Vol. III, P. 207]

485 cont'd

a cont'd

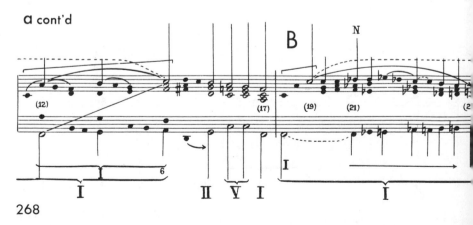

268

484 cont'd

ı cont'd

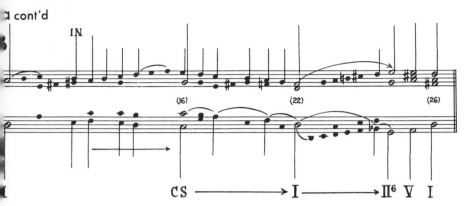

CS ⟶ I ⟶ II⁶ V I

485 BRAHMS Feldeinsamkeit

a

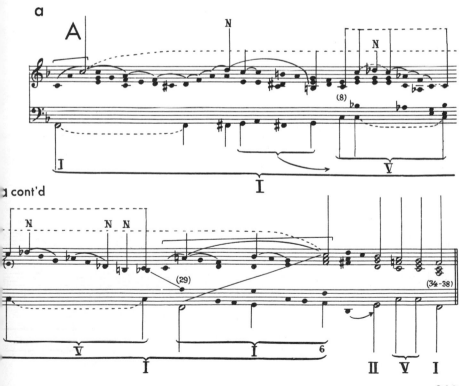

ı cont'd

486 # FRESCOBALDI La Frescobalda

[From *EPM*, P. 33]

a

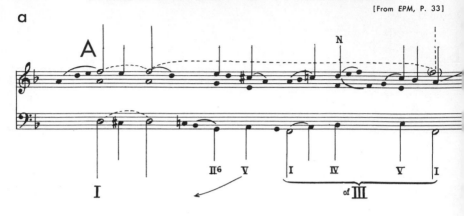

b

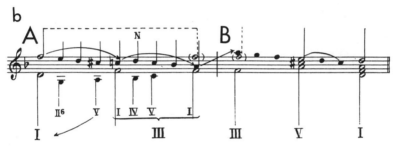

487 # D. SCARLATTI Sonata, G Major, L. 490

a

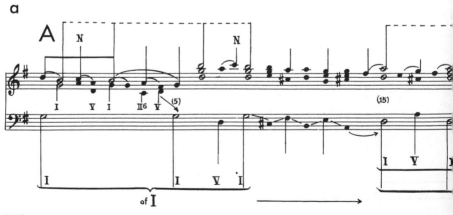

486 cont'd

cont'd

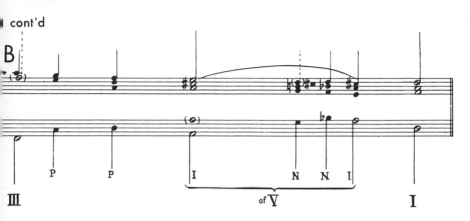

487 cont'd

cont'd

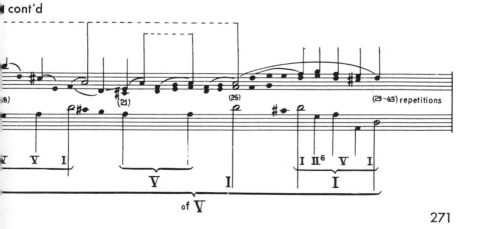

487 cont'd

488 WOLF In der Frühe

487 cont'd

a cont'd

488 cont'd

a cont'd

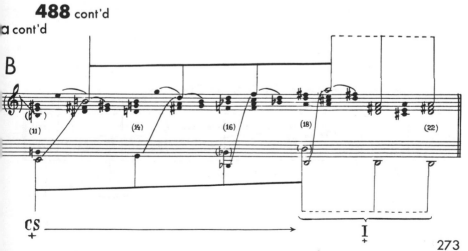

488 cont'd

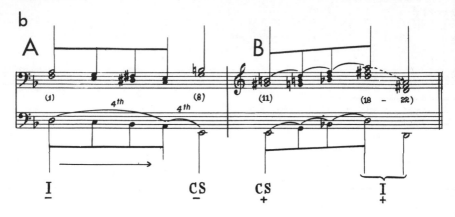

489 HINDEMITH Interludium (Ludus Tonalis)

meas. 19 - 24 similar to meas. 5 -10

488 cont'd

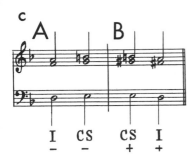

c

A   B

I   CS   CS   I
—   —   +   +

489 cont'd

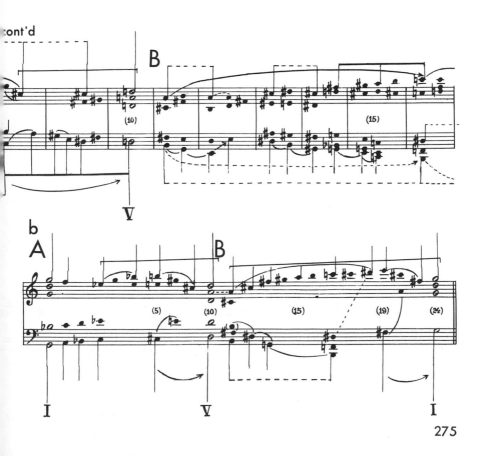

cont'd

B

(10)   (15)

V

b

A   B

(5)   (10)   (15)   (19)   (24)

I   V   I

489cont'd

c

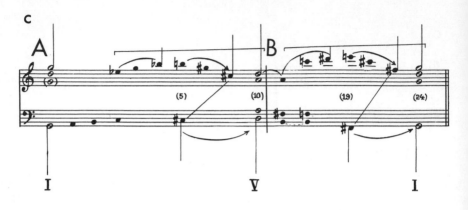

e

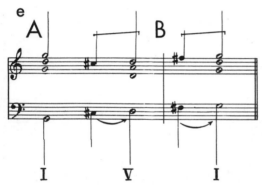

490 BYRD Pavane: The Earle of
Salisbury

a

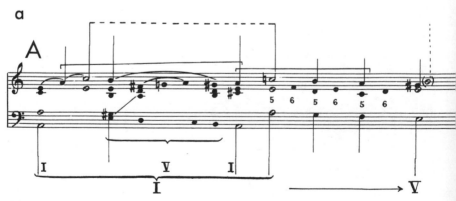

489 cont'd

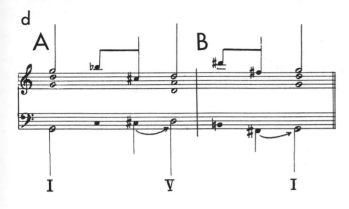

490 cont'd

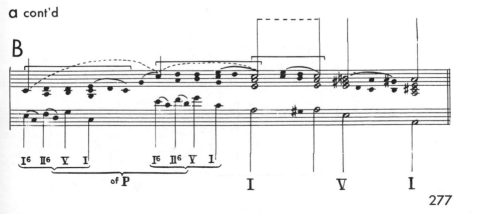

490 cont'd

b

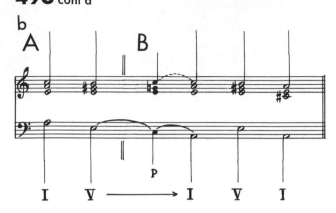

I   V ⟶ I   V   I

491   BEETHOVEN String Quartet, Op 18, No. 5. 3rd movement

a

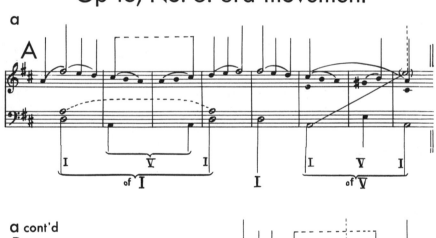

a cont'd

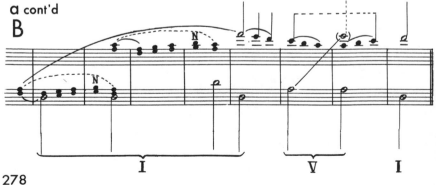

491 cont'd

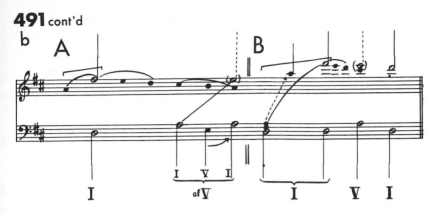

492   CHOPIN Prelude, Op 28, No. 1

493 BACH Little Prelude, G minor

494 BRAHMS Waltz, Op 39, No. 8

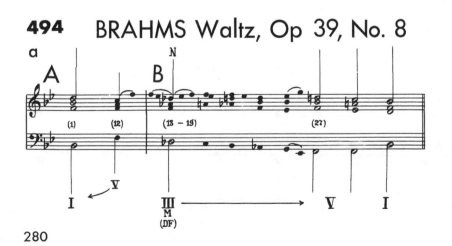

493 cont'd

nt'd

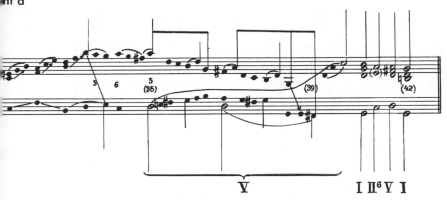

495 BACH Minuet 2 (Partita No. 1)

496

a

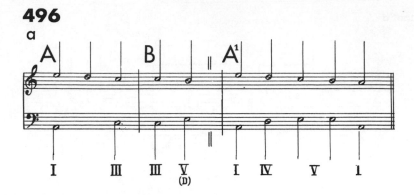

497 SCHUBERT Symphony, B minor.
1st movement

a

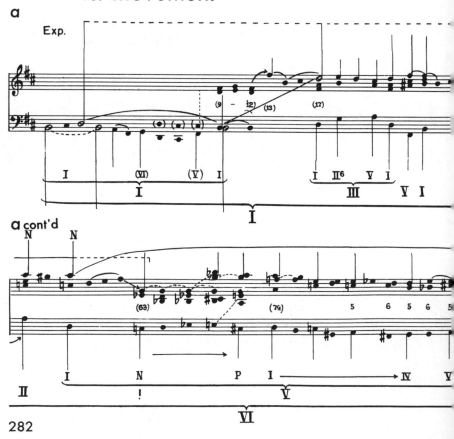

a cont'd

496 cont'd

b

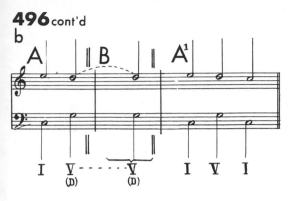

497 cont'd

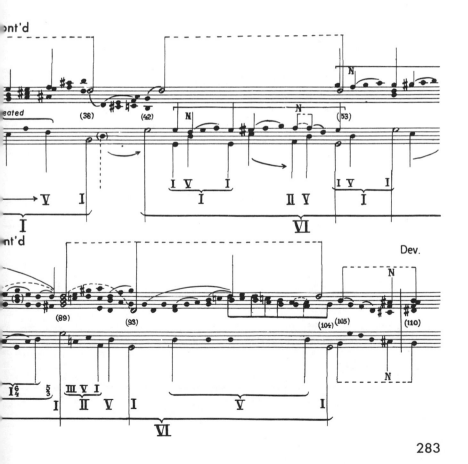

a cont'd

Dev.

a cont'd

a cont'd

497 cont'd

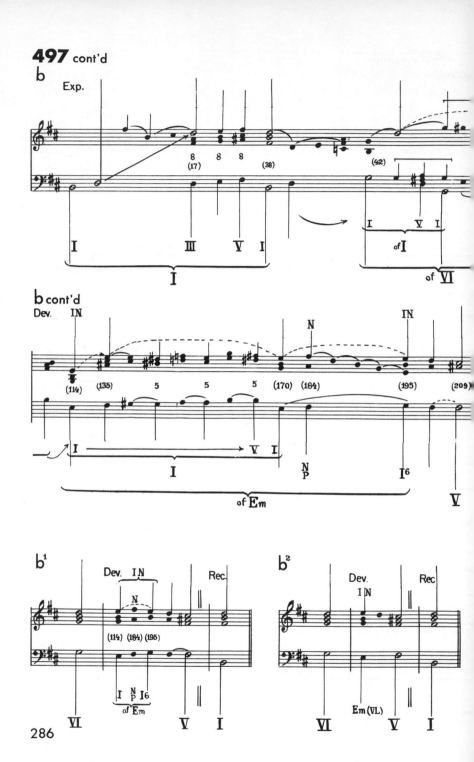

286

ont'd

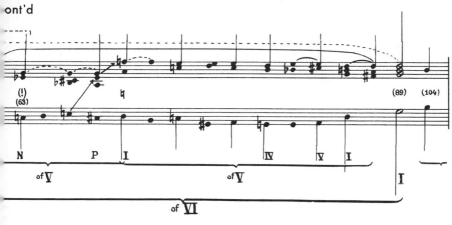

ont'd

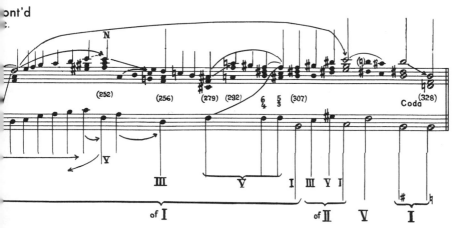

C

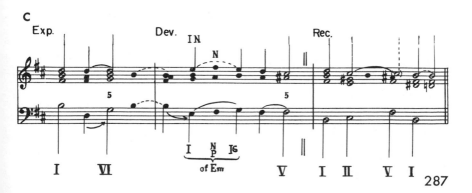

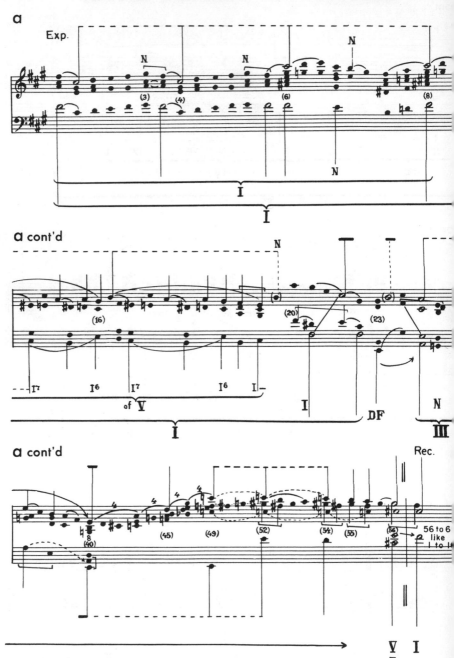

498 cont'd

500 CHOPIN Nocturne, Op 9, No. 2

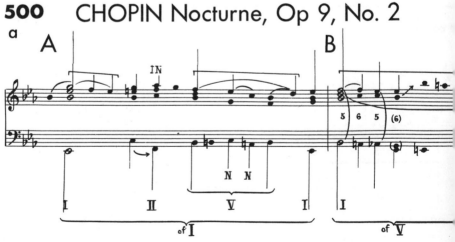

498 cont'd

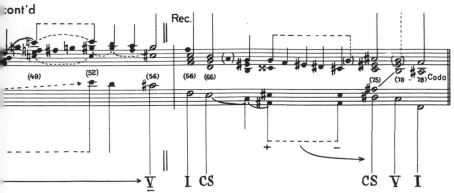

499 CHOPIN Mazurka, Op 17, No. 2

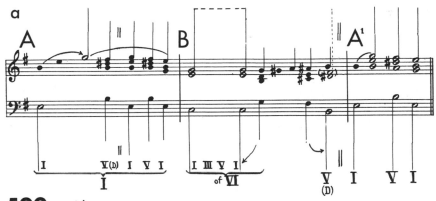

500 cont'd

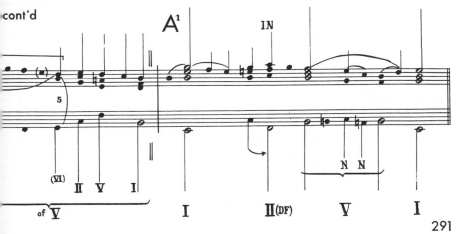

500 cont'd

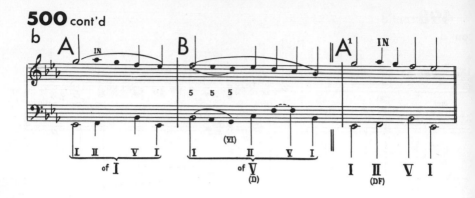

501 cont'd

a cont'd

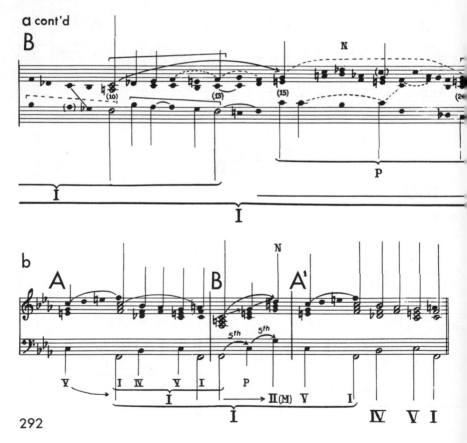

292

501 MONTEVERDI Madrigal: Lasciatemi morire

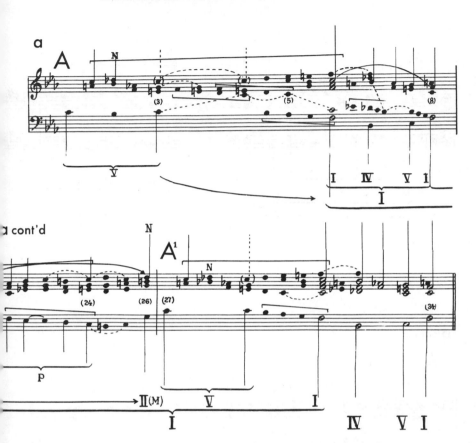

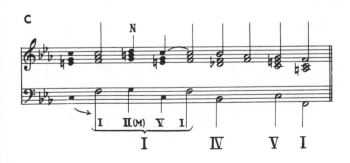

a

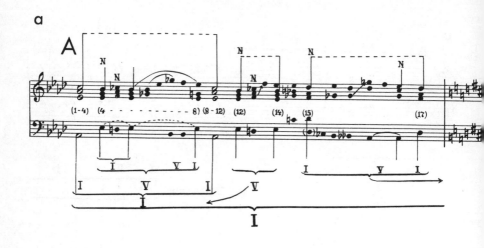

a cont'd

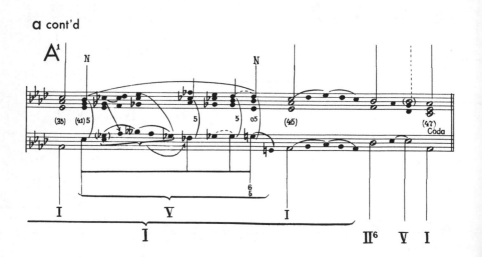

cont'd

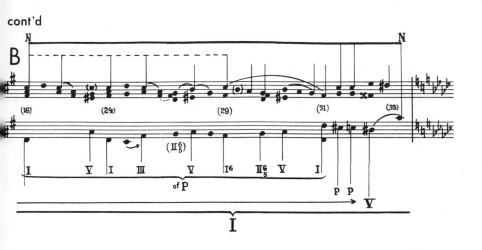

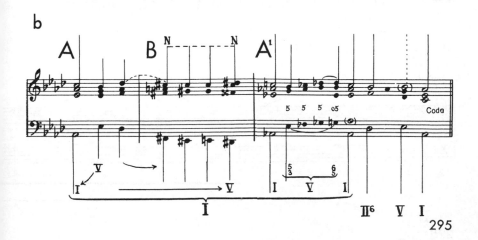

503 BRAHMS Symphony No. 3. 1st movement

a

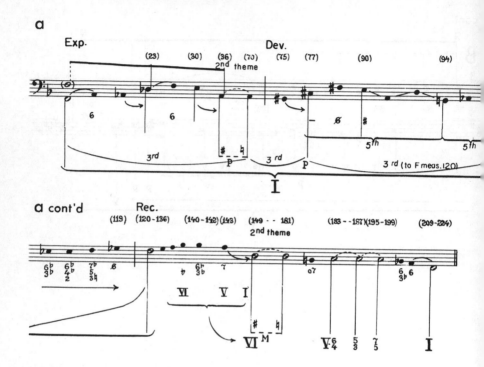

a cont'd

504 BARTÓK Bourrée (Mikrokosmos, Bk IV)

a

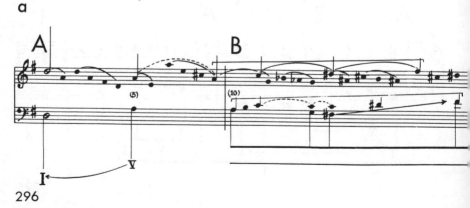

503 cont'd

a cont'd

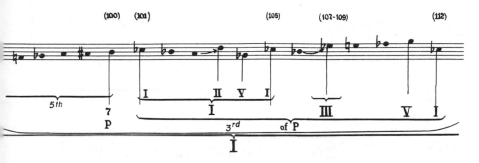

b

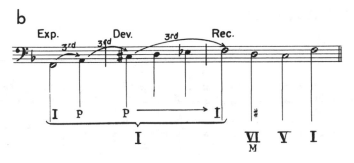

504 cont'd

a cont'd

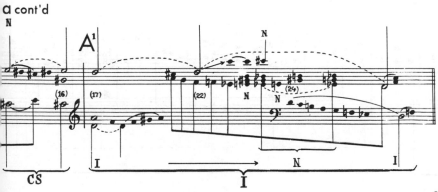

504 cont'd

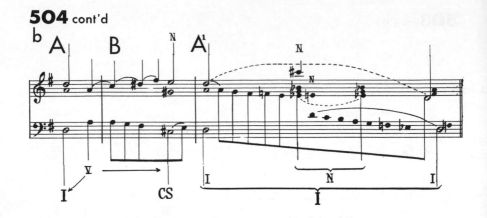

505 HINDEMITH Piano Sonata No. 2
1st movement

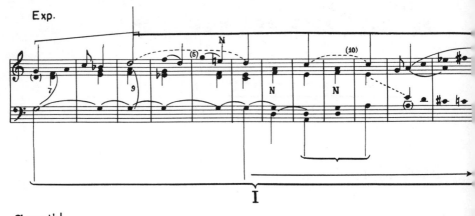

a cont'd transition

to F meas. 36-41

504 cont'd

C

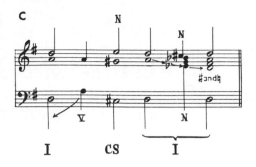

505 cont'd

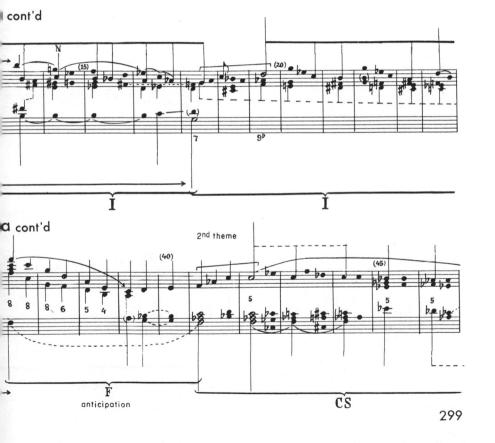

505 cont'd

a cont'd

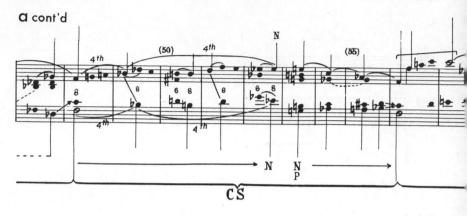

a cont'd

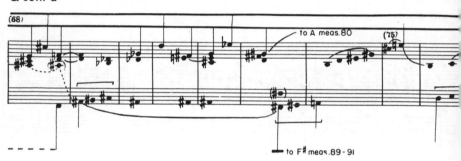

a cont'd

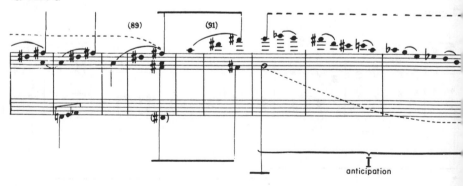

505 cont'd

cont'd

Dev.

via F# to G (meas. 95)

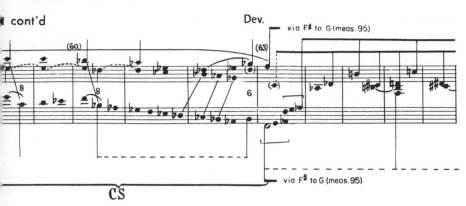

CS

cont'd

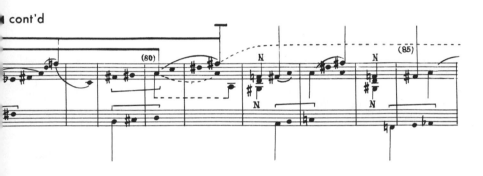

cont'd
Rec.

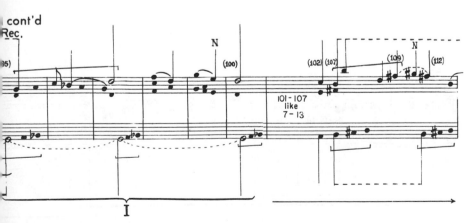

101 - 107
like
7 - 13

I

505 cont'd

a cont'd

(113)   (115)   (120)

Canonic imitation

CS

a cont'd

(136)   (139)   (140)

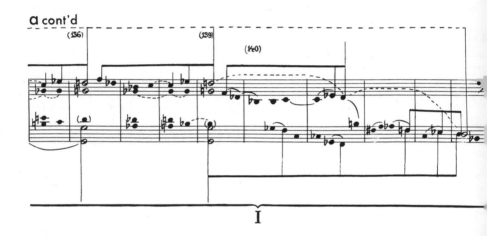

I

b

Exp.
1st theme

transition

(8-10)   (17)   (26)

8ve

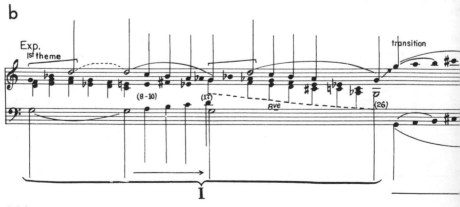

I

cont'd

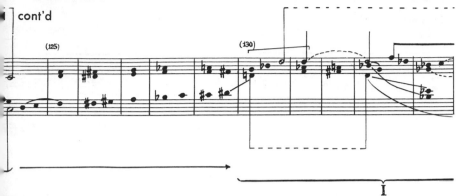

(125)   (130)

I

cont'd

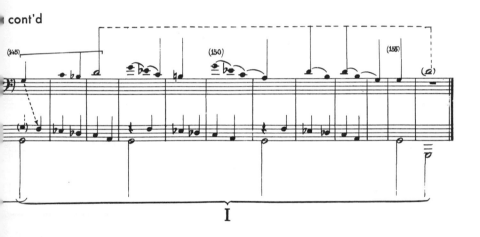

(145)   (150)   (155)   (2)

I

cont'd

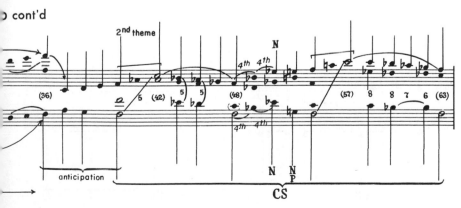

2nd theme

N

4th 4th

(36)   2 5 (42) 5 5 (48)   (57) 8 8 7 6 (63)

4th 4th

anticipation

N   N
    P

CS

505 cont'd

b cont'd
Dev.

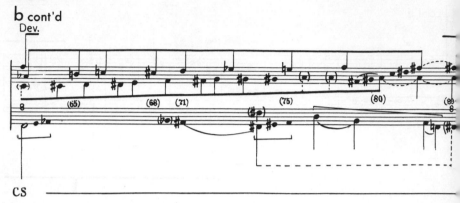

(65) (68) (71) (75) (80) (85)

CS

c
A

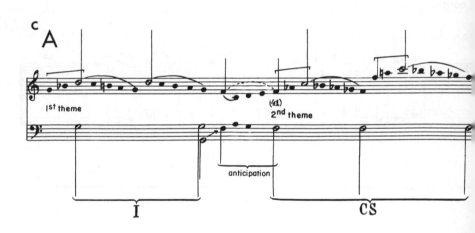

1st theme

(41)
2nd theme

anticipation

I

CS

d
A   **B**   **A¹**

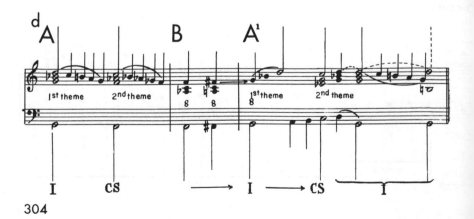

1st theme   2nd theme   1st theme   2nd theme

I   CS   → I → CS   I

505 cont'd

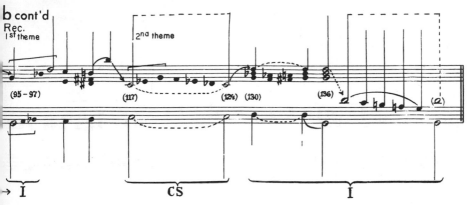

b cont'd
Rec.
1st theme   2nd theme

(95–97)   (117)   (124) (130)   (136)   (2)

→ I   CS   I

c cont'd
B   **A¹**

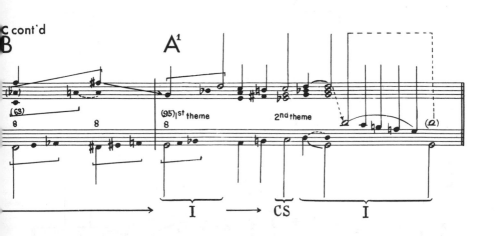

(63)   (95) 1st theme   2nd theme   (2)
8   8   8

⟶   I ⟶ CS   I

e

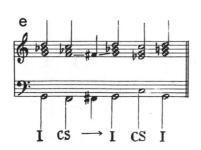

I CS ⟶ I CS I

f

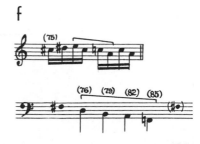

(75)

(76) (79) (82) (85)

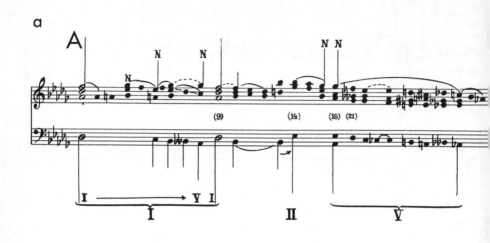

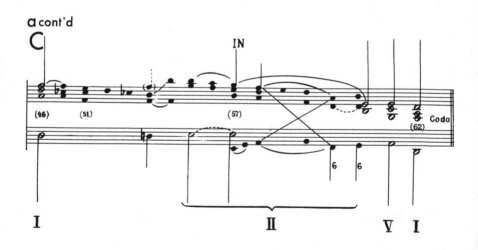

cont'd

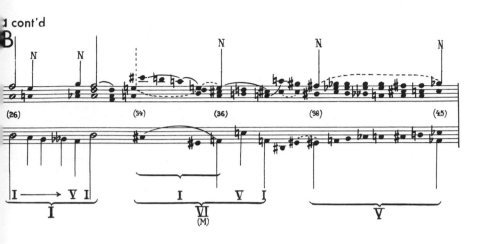

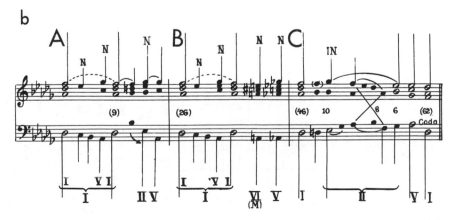

507 MOZART Fantasia, C minor, K. 475

a
Adagio

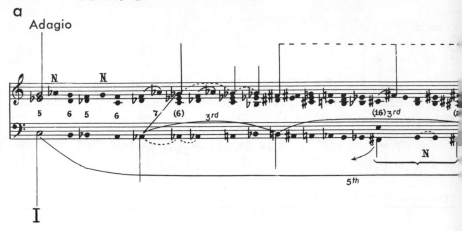

a cont'd
Allegro

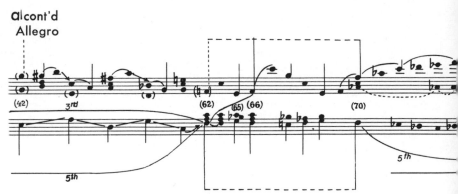

a cont'd
Andantino

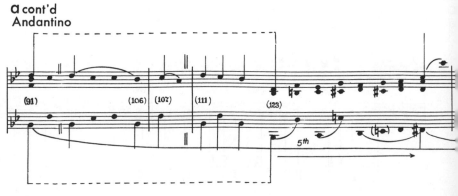

ɔ cont'd

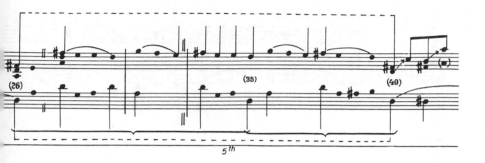

ɑ cont'd

ɑ cont'd

Più Allegro

⌐ to Aᵇ meas. 143

a cont'd

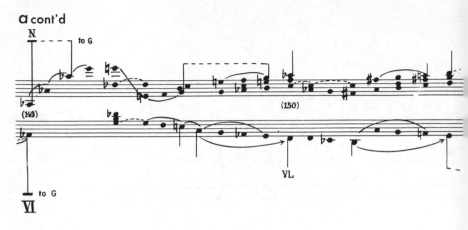

b

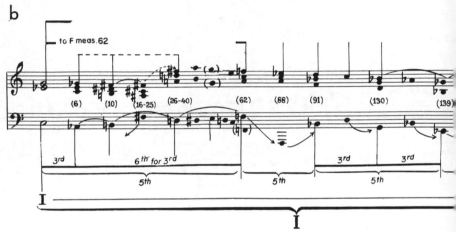

c

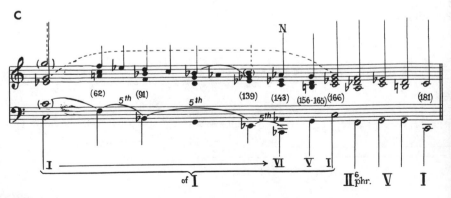

cont'd

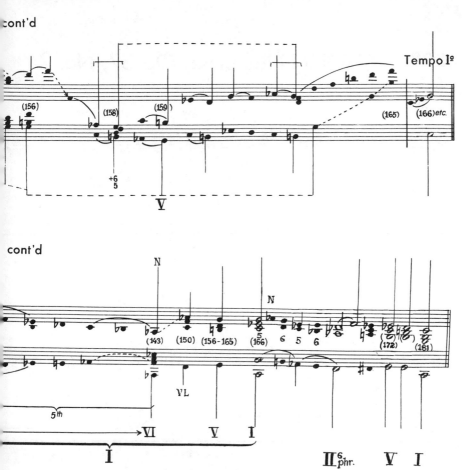

cont'd

508 CHOPIN Nocturne, Op 37, No. 2

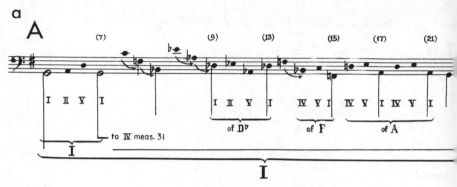

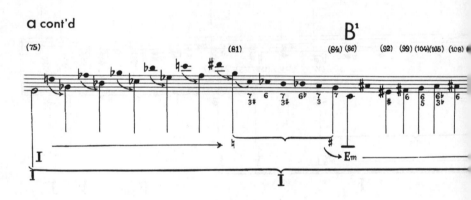

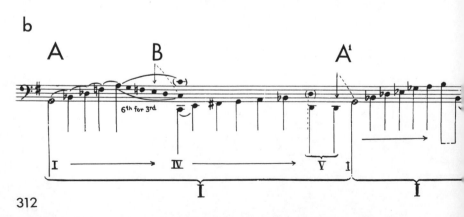

508 cont'd

cont'd

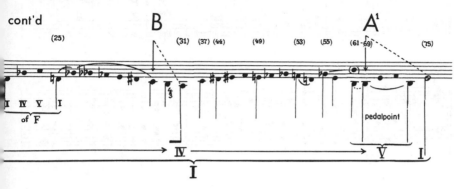

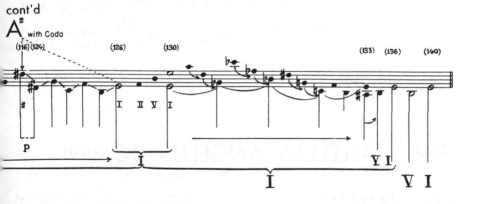

cont'd

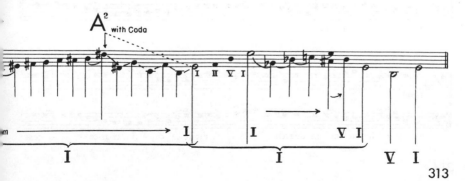

509 LASSO Christe Dei soboles

Chri - ste, de - i so - bo - les, spes ___ et ___ me - a so -

la vo - lu - ptas, etc.

etc.

[From *HDM*, Vol. I, P. 333]

Part III Chapter Two

510 ALLELUIA ANGELUS DOMINI

(Solo)

(Chorus)

Al - le - - lu - ia. Al - le - - lu - ia.

(Solo)

An - ge - lus do - mi - ni de-scen - - - - - dit de ___ ce - lo: et ac-ce - - - dens

510 cont'd

re-vol - - - - vit la - - - pi-dem et — se-de-bat su-per e-um. ____

[From *HAM*, Vol. I, No. 26c]

511 BENEDICAMUS DOMINO
(School of St. Martial)

Be - - - - - - - - - - ne - - - - - - - - - -

etc.

di - - - - - - - - - - - - - ca - - - - - - mus ____

[From *HDM*, Vol. I, P. 179]

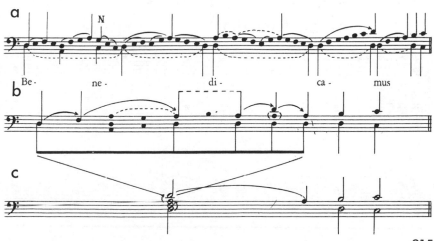

a

N

b

Be - ne - di - ca - mus

c

512 **BENEDICAT ERGO (School of Compostela)**

Be - ne - di - cat er - go plebs fi - de - - - lis
do - - - - - - - - - - - - - - - - mi - no

[From *HDM*, Vol. I, P. 182]

a

a cont'd

513 **VIDERUNT HEMANUEL (School of St. Martial)**

Vi - de - - runt _____ He - - ma - nu - - - - - - - el

[From *HAM*, Vol. I, No. 27a]

a

C?
G

514   LEONINUS Alleluia Pascha

Alleluia, etc.

[From AUDM, PP. 94-95]

515 ORGANUM (Style of Perotinus)

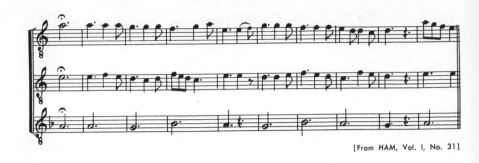

[From *HAM*, Vol. I, No. 31]

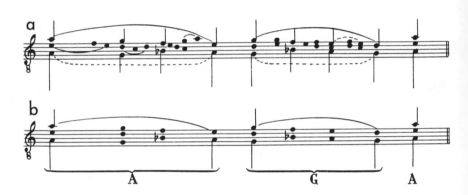

a

b

A   G   A

516 PEROTINUS Organum Triplum

Na

[From HDM, Vol. I, P. 226]

516 cont'd

a

A

a cont'd

G F

517 MOTET

O Ma - ri - a, vir - go da - vi - di - ca,   Vir - gi - num flos vi - tae spes u - ni - ca

O Ma - ri - a, ma - ris stel - la, Ple - na gra - ti - ae

(Veritatem)

[From MMA, P. 316]

a

U.N   L.N

F

b

F

516 cont'd

cont'd

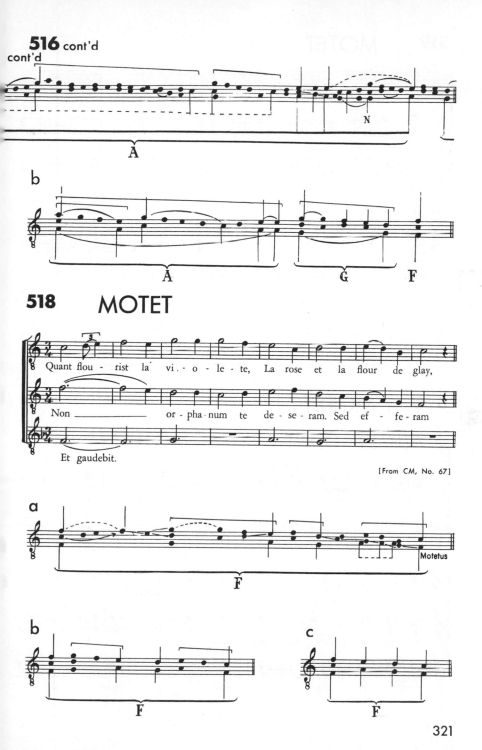

N

A

b

A G F

518 MOTET

Quant flou - rist la vi - o - le - te, La rose et la flour de glay,

Non _____ or - pha - num te de - se - ram. Sed ef - fe - ram

Et gaudebit.

[From CM, No. 67]

a

Motetus

F

b c

F F

519 MOTET

Sed ho - mi - - - num in - ter tot mi - li - a

Qui to - ci - - - us vi - res in - ge - ni - i

(Egregie)

a

[From CM, No. 79]

A

b

Motetus   Triplum   Motetus   both

A

520 MOTET

Qui a - mours vuelt main - te - nir Et — ser - vir Lo - iau - - ment sans faus -

Li dous pen - - ser — Qui mi vient de ce - li

Cis a cui je sui a - mi - e Est

ser,   Bien se _ doit sour tou - te riens gar - der

Que J'aim de cuer, _ Car tous jours l'ai ser - - vi _ Sans gui -

preux — et gais,   Pour s'a - mour se -

322

520 cont'd

De vi - la - ni - e, Qui — tant fait a blas - - mer,

ler, Et bons es - - poirs que j'ai d'avoir

rai jo - li - - e Tant com vi - - vrai.

[From CM, No. 54]

a

b

Melodic outline

521 MOTET

O Ma - ri - - a, re - gi - - na — glo - ri - - -

Au - - di, Pa - - ter, sal - va nos, tu qui

Alleluya

e, Fons in - dul - - gen - ci - - e, Tu - - um, Ma -

es Sa - lus et — re - qui - - es Et re - ple —

323

521 cont'd

ter, ex- o - - ra ____ Fi - li - - um, Ut pro no - -

nos spi - ri - tu di - vi - - no, Ut ____ gra - ci - -

a

b

522 MOTET

L'au - tre jour par un ma - - - ti - net M'en ____ a - -

Hier ____ ma - ti - net Trou - vai sans son

Omnes,

lai - es be - ni - ant Et trou - vai sans son ber - ge - ret

ber - ge - - ret Pas - toure es - ga - re - - - - e;

[From CM, No. 40]

324

bis ex - o - - - ret ____ Do - mi - - - - - num.

as a - ga - - - mus ____ Do - mi - - - - - no.

a cont'd

[From CM, No. 9]

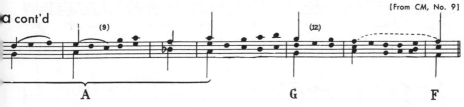

A   G   F

522 cont'd

a

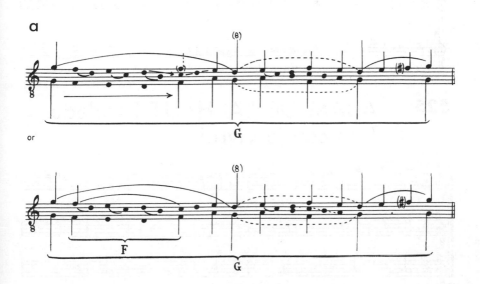

or

G

F

G

523 RONDEAU: Amours et ma dame aussi

A-mours et ma dame aus - - si   jointes mains vous   proi mer - chi!
etc.

[From MMA, P. 322]

a

524 ADAM DE LA HALLE Li maus d'amer (1st part)

Li maus   d'a - - - mer   me plaist miex _ a   sen - - - - - tir

K'a main-ta - mant ne ___ fait li dons ___ de ___ joi - - e, ___ etc.

[From HAM, Vol. I, No. 36a]

525 ADAM DE LA HALLE Rondeau: Tant con je vivrai

Tant ___ con   je ___ vi - - - - vrai   N'a - me - - - -

525 cont'd

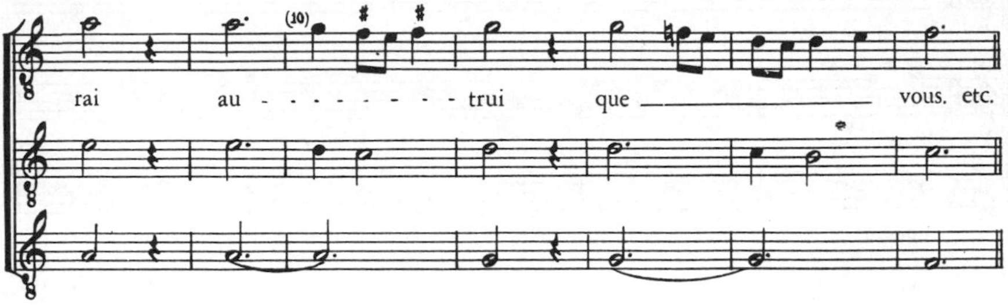

[From *HAM*, Vol. I, No. 36b]

a

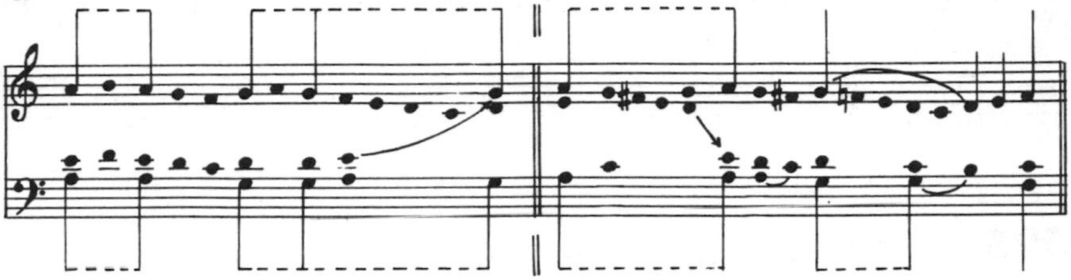

526 MOTET

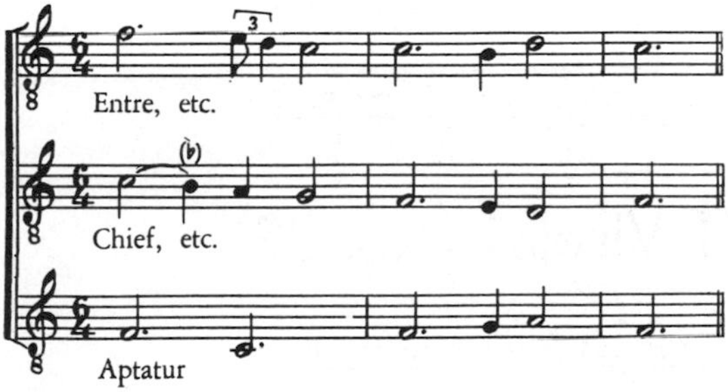

[From *CM*, No. 24]

a

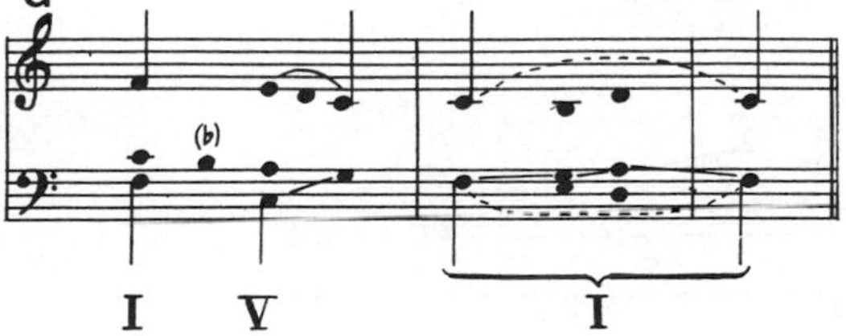

527 MOTET

Au dous, etc.

Biaus, etc.

Manere

[From CM, No. 18]

a

I → V   I

528 MACHAUT Virelai (No. 38)

De _ tout.sui si   con - for - - - te - e

[From MW, Vol. I]

a

I → V   I

529 MACHAUT Virelai (No. 32)

Da - me   mon _ cuer em - por - - tes

[From MW, Vol. I]

a

I V   I   V   I
I

530 MACHAUT Ballade (No. 3)

(flour etc.)

[From MW, Vol. I]

a

b

I

$\underset{\text{(III?)}}{\text{C S}} \rightarrow$ V I

531 MACHAUT Rondeau (No. 13)

Da - me, — se — vous n'a - vez a - per - ce - u

que — je vous aim de — cuer, etc.

[From MW, Vol. I]

a

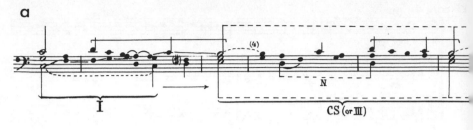

b

532   MACHAUT Virelai (No. 31)

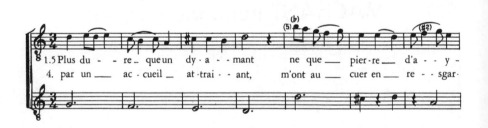

1.5 Plus du - - re _ que un dy - a - - mant   ne que __ pier - re __ d'a - - y -
4. par un __ ac - cueil _ at -trai - - ant,   m'ont au __ cuer en __ re - -sgar-

mant est __ vo dur - - té,   da - me qui __ n'a - ves pi - - té, de __
dant si __ fort na - -vré   que __ ja - mais __ joi - e n'a - -vré, ju - -

531 cont'd

a cont'd

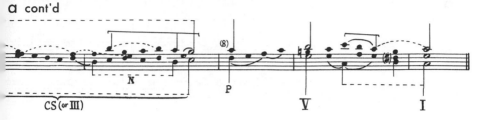

CS (or III)   N   P   V   I

532 cont'd

vostre a - - mant qu'o ci - - - es en __ de - - si - rant vostre __ a - mi - - tié.

sques a - - tant que vo __ gra-ce __ quïl __ a - tant m'au - - res don - - né.

2. Da - me, __ vo pu - - re __ biau - té   qui __ tou - tes __ passe, __

3. simple et __ plein d'u - - mi - li - té,   de __ dou - ceur __ fi - -

a - mon - gré, et __ vo __ sam - blant   ré, en __ sous ri - - - ant,

ne __ pa -

[From MW, Vol. I]

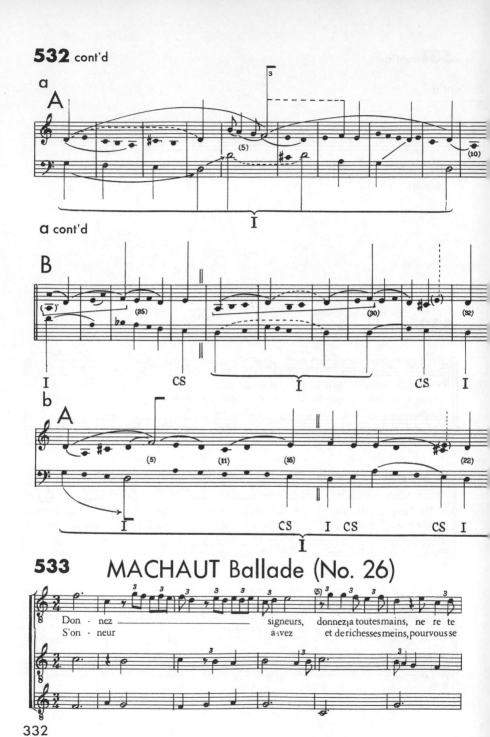

533 MACHAUT Ballade (No. 26)

Don · nez _____ signeurs, donnez ja toutes mains, ne re te
S'on · neur a · vez et de richesses meins, pour vous se

533 cont'd

l'on - neur.
me - neur

cha - - scuns _ di - -

ra: _ ci a vaillant si-gneur. Et terre aus-siqu'est despen.....du------e

a

A

(3) (6) N (9)

I
I

a cont'd

B

(18) (21) (24)

I
I

vaut trop mieus que ter - - re per - - du - - - - - - - - - - - - - e

[From MW, Vol. I]

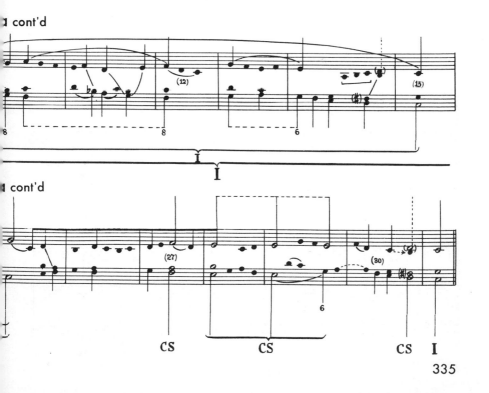

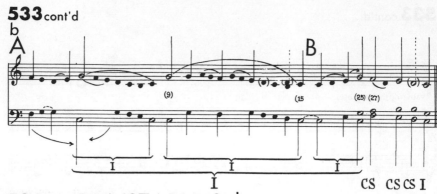

534 DUNSTABLE Sub tuam protectionem

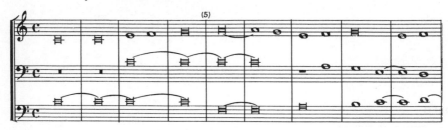

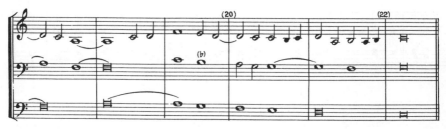

[From *TC*, Vol. I, P. 198]

534 cont'd

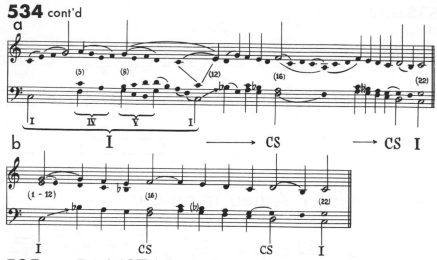

a

(5)   (8)   (12)   (16)   (22)

I   IV   V   I

I   ——→ CS   ——→ CS   I

b

(1 - 12)   (16)   (22)

I   CS   CS   I

535   DUNSTABLE Puisque m'amour

(5)

Puis-que m'a mour _ m'a _ pris en _____ des - - - - - - plai-

(10)

sir

(15)   (19)

[From TC, Vol. I. P. 254]

337

535 cont'd

a

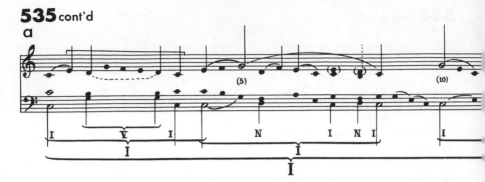

536 DUFAY Adieu m'amour

A ‑ ‑ ‑ dieu m'a ‑ ‑ mour, ‑ a ‑ ‑ ‑ dieu ‑ ma ıoy ‑ ‑ ‑

A ‑ dieu ‑‑‑ m'a ‑ mour, a ‑ ‑ dieu ‑ ma ioy ‑ ‑ ‑ ‑

e, A ‑ dieu le so ‑ las que i'a ‑ voy ‑ ‑ ‑ ‑ ‑ ‑ ‑ ‑

e, A ‑ dieu le so ‑ las que i'a ‑ voy ‑ ‑ ‑ ‑ ‑ ‑ ‑ ‑ ‑

‑ ‑ ‑ ‑ e, A ‑ dieu ma le ‑ a ‑ le mais ‑ tres ‑ ‑ ‑ ‑ se.

‑ ‑ ‑ ‑ e, ‑‑‑ A ‑ dieu ma ‑ le ‑ a ‑ le mais ‑ tres ‑ ‑ ‑ ‑ se.

535 cont'd

a cont'd

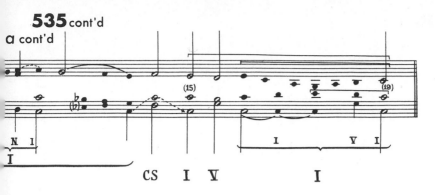

536 cont'd

Le di - re a dieu tant _ fort _ me bles - - - - - - se

Le di - re a-dieu tant _ fort me bles - - - - - - - se_

Qu'il me sam - ble que mo - rir doy - - - - - - - - - -

_ Qu'il me sam - ble que mo - rir doy - - - - - - - - - -

e

e.

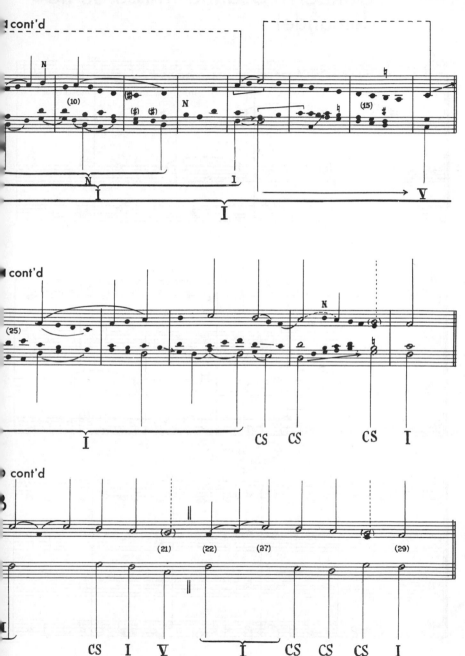

537   OBRECHT Osanna (Missa: Je ne demande)

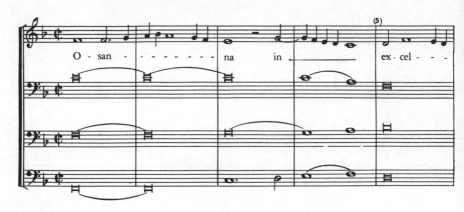

O - san - - - - - - - - na in _____ ex - cel - - -

- - - - - - - sis,   etc.

537cont'd

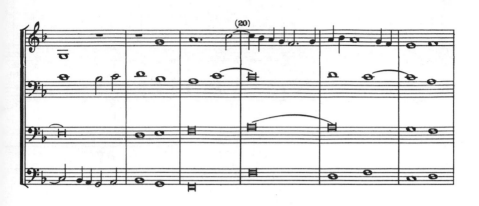

[From *WJO, Missen,* Vol. 1, No. 1]

a

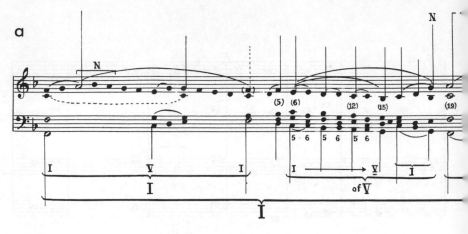

b

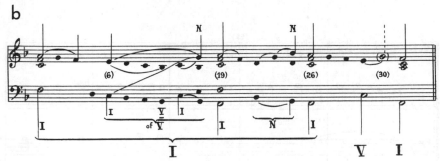

538   ISAAC Kyrie (Missa Carminum)

Ky — ri — — — e — e — lei — — son, etc.

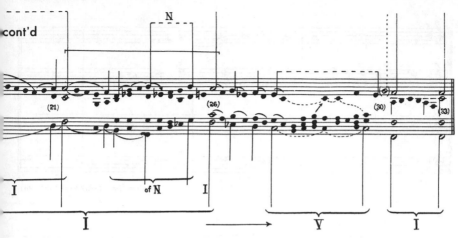

538 cont'd

a

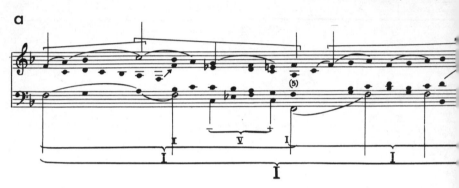

539 # JOSQUIN Motet: O Domine Jesu Christe (1st part)

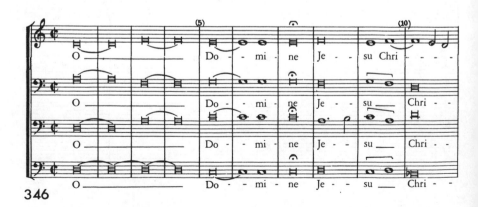

538 cont'd

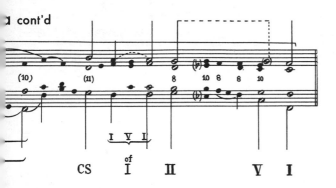

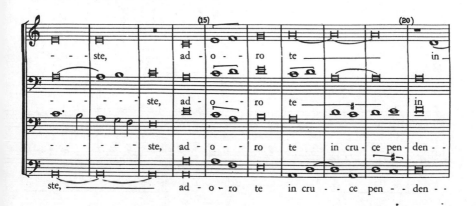

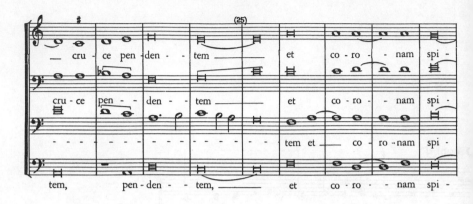

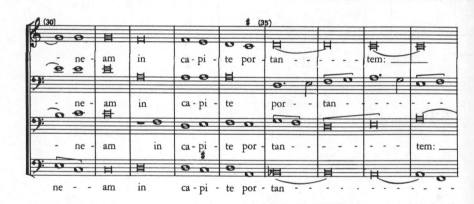

a

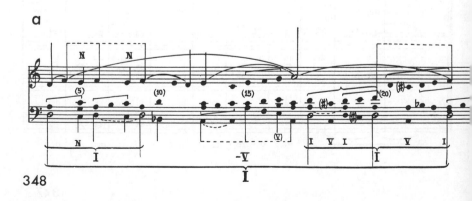

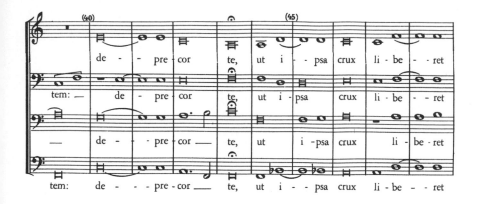

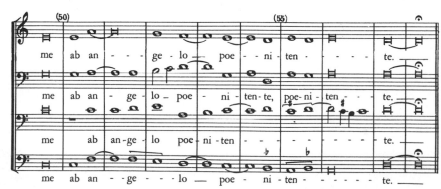

[From *WJP, Motetten*, Vol. II, P. 35]

a cont'd

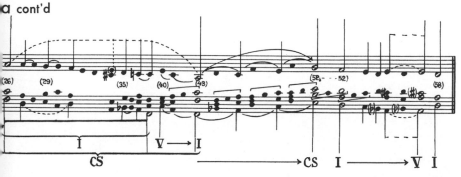